You Won't Believe Your Eyes!

BOOKS FOR WORLD EXPLORERS
NATIONAL GEOGRAPHIC SOCIETY

Contents

COVER AND TITLE PAGE: *If you're baffled by the girls' change in size, this fact may confuse you even more: The girls are two of a set of identical triplets. They're Stacy (in white shoes) and Julie Saal, 13, from Larkspur, California. What's peculiar is the room. It isn't what it seems. The Distorted Room Exhibit amazes visitors to the Exploratorium, a hands-on science museum in San Francisco. An explanation of the illusion begins on page 7.*
PHIL SCHERMEISTER

▷ *At first glance, this room too may seem quite ordinary. But the girl looking through the door would have to be a giant for the room to be of normal size. She's Alissa Grad, 8, of Kings Point, New York. When you look even closer, you see that the room is not just a miniature—it's an aquarium. You can usually believe your eyes, but, as you're discovering, not always.*

1

A World of Illusions

What's going on here? Did an earthquake tilt these houses and crinkle the sidewalk? At first glance you might think so, but take a closer look. Things are just a bit too orderly. The scene is an illusion. This is San Francisco, California, a city built on hills. The girl is actually coasting down a hill so steep that the sidewalk consists of stairsteps. To create the illusion, the photographer tilted his camera to the left. The hill became horizontal. A false visual clue such as this one can cause the brain to misread a scene. If you were fooled by what you saw here, it's understandable. The world as we see it is full of illusions. As you'll discover, what you see is not necessarily what you get.

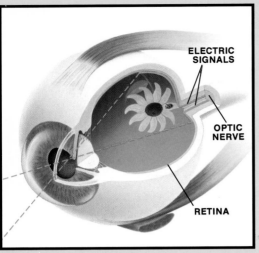

ELECTRIC
SIGNALS

OPTIC
NERVE

RETINA

◁ *An image on the retina (RET-nuh) has no depth and is inverted. The image shrinks as the object moves farther away. Because each eye views an object from a different position, the two retinal images differ slightly. The small difference in viewpoint helps your brain judge distance.*

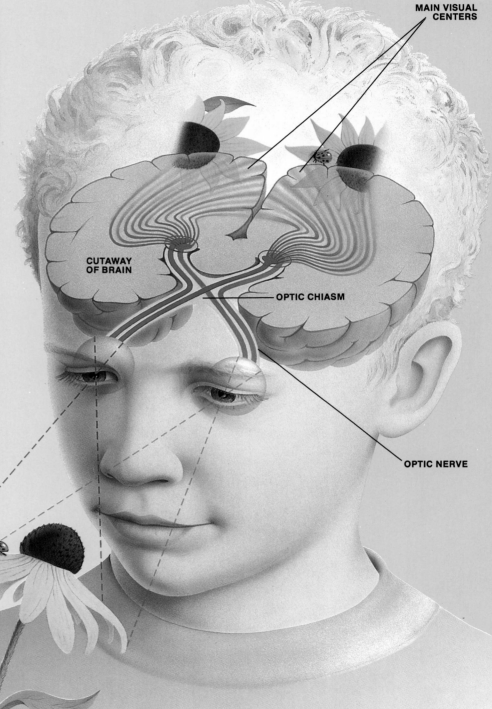

MAIN VISUAL
CENTERS

CUTAWAY
OF BRAIN

OPTIC CHIASM

OPTIC NERVE

*Tops in teamwork: Your eyes link up with your brain to give you vision **(right)**. Light reflected from an object—here a flower—enters each eye. The light is focused as an image on the retina **(above)**, the inside surface of the eyeball. There, the light is converted into electric impulses—signals for the brain. The impulses travel toward the brain along the optic nerves. On the way, half of each optic nerve crosses over at the optic chiasm (KIE-az-um). The main visual center in each side of the brain thus receives impulses from both eyes. The brain combines and interprets the impulses, seeking clues as to form, size, color, and depth. Finally, the brain comes up with its best guess as to what the information means. That guess is what you see.*

JANE HURD

— — — — — **RIGHT–EYE FIELD**

— — — — — **LEFT–EYE FIELD**

6

When a family goes on vacation, someone is sure to take a camera along. If the trip takes the family to a spectacular place—such as the Grand Canyon or a forest of giant redwood trees—the family photographer may ask someone to get in the picture to show just how big things really are.

By providing a size comparison, the person adds an important visual clue to the scene. One clue can completely change the way you see something. Look at the picture on pages 14–15. At first, you'll probably think you're seeing a real historic landmark. But study the picture more closely. A clue in the picture's lower right corner tells you that you're looking at something quite different.

To perceive, or understand, the visible world, your brain needs information, or clues. Two sources feed visual information to the brain: the eyes, and the brain's memory of past experience. Usually the information is clear enough. You have no difficulty figuring out what you're looking at.

Sometimes, however, the information is faulty. Maybe there's not enough of it—or there's too much. Perhaps nothing in your experience can help your brain interpret the clues that come to it. When the information is faulty, your brain may come up with a wrong guess about what it thinks it sees. You experience a visual illusion.

Your eyes and brain together form a visual system (opposite page). The eyes gather light reflected from an *object*. Each eye focuses the light as an *image* on the retina. The retina is a lining containing light-sensitive cells. It covers most of the inner surface of the eyeball. The retinal image is two-dimensional, or flat. It has height and width but no depth.

Cells in each retina change each image into electric signals, a code the brain understands. The brain sorts, selects, arranges, and rearranges the signals. It considers input from the other senses and figures out depth. Finally, the brain comes up with the "best bet." It's a guess—and it is what you see.

Seen often enough, an object becomes a familiar pattern to the brain. Once the pattern is memorized, the brain tends to identify that pattern with a particular kind of object. That's why your brain sees the room on the cover of this book as "normal." *Something* is peculiar, though. The *(Continued on page 11)*

▷ *Put your visual powers to work to put this fish back into its bowl. Stare at the fish for about 30 seconds. Then shift your gaze to the bowl. In a few seconds, the fish will reappear—but in different colors. This is what happens. It always takes awhile for a retinal image to fade. When you look away, an afterimage remains on each retina. Here, too much exposure dulls the retinal cells sensitive to red and yellow. They stop sending red and yellow signals to the brain. In the absence of these colors, you see their opposites. The fish in the bowl becomes green and violet.*
MARVIN J. FRYER

7

Fooling the Eye With Lines, Circles, and Colors

The illusions on these two pages will do more than entertain you. They'll show you that seeing is really problem solving. Illusions result when the brain comes up with a wrong or incomplete solution to a set of clues. What you *think* you see is not what's really there.

Scientists use illusions like these to discover how the brain allows itself to be fooled. Can *you* be fooled? Look at the shapes at lower right. You probably think you see a pair of overlapping triangles. Look again. The brain has added lines where there are none—and you see triangles where they do not exist. By the time you're ready to turn the page, you may not be so ready to believe your eyes!

△ Monument or bridge? As solid as it looks at first glance, this structure could never be built. It's an impossible figure. Try following the columns from top to bottom. It gets confusing. Does the structure have two columns—or three?

△ Which butterfly outline is red? Remarkably, they both are—and the same shade, at that. Surrounding colors affect how you perceive a color. In this case, the green acts to strengthen the red. The violet tends to make the red look orange.

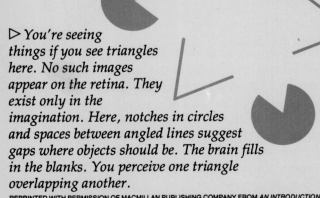

▷ You're seeing things if you see triangles here. No such images appear on the retina. They exist only in the imagination. Here, notches in circles and spaces between angled lines suggest gaps where objects should be. The brain fills in the blanks. You perceive one triangle overlapping another.

△ If the off-center circle were a coin, would it roll? By its lopsided appearance, you might think not. In fact, it's a perfect circle. The angles formed by the lines coming out of the center of the larger circle confuse your brain into thinking it sees an irregular shape. Doubt it? Place a 50-cent piece in the circle and see for yourself.

REPRINTED WITH PERMISSION OF MACMILLAN PUBLISHING COMPANY FROM *AN INTRODUCTION TO PERCEPTION*, BY IRVIN ROCK. COPYRIGHT © 1975 BY IRVIN ROCK.

▷ Indian chief or Eskimo? You'll see one or the other right away. Suddenly, your perception of the drawing will shift, and you'll see a different figure. The drawing is ambiguous—that is, you can interpret it in different ways.

FROM *ILLUSION IN NATURE AND ART*, EDITED BY R. L. GREGORY AND E. H. GOMBRICH, PUBLISHED BY DUCKWORTH.

▽ This painting may make you think you're peering into a whirlpool. But the split lines are actually perfect circles, not a spiral. The blue and yellow line segments curve toward the center. Searching for a continuous pattern, the brain sees a spiral rather than a series of interrupted circles.

FROM *SEEING*, BY JOHN FRISBY, PUBLISHED BY OXFORD UNIVERSITY PRESS. PHOTO COPYRIGHT © BRIAN WRIGHT/AUGUSTINE STUDIOS.

△ The long and the short of it: If you measure the green lines, you may be astonished to find that they're of equal length. By using converging lines—lines that tend toward one another—the artist has created the illusion of depth. That "depth" tricks you into thinking the "far" line, which runs from floor to ceiling, must be longer than the "near" line, which doesn't.

MARVIN J. FRYER

(Continued from page 7) girl standing in the left corner appears unnaturally small in comparison with the other girl.

Actually, the girls are the same size. The room is *not* normal. It is odd-shaped. The left corner is twice as far away from the viewer as the right. The ceiling slopes down toward the right corner; the floor slopes up toward it.

You perceive none of that, though. That's because the room forms the same image on the retina as a rectangular room would. The brain must make a decision: Is the room an odd shape, or is one girl much shorter than the other? Since both girls *appear* to be at the same distance from the observer, the brain chooses to see the room as normal. It may be the best bet—but it's the wrong one.

Scientists generally divide illusions into two types, *cognitive* and *physiological*. Cognitive illusions involve experience and assumptions. In the Distorted Room illusion, the messages from the retinal image of the room match up with stored information about rectangular rooms. You therefore assume the room to be rectangular. There is no reason to assume differently; nothing suggests that one girl might actually be farther away than the other.

Physiological illusions are "hardware"

illusions. They are caused by disturbances of the circuits of the eye-brain system. The paintings on these pages rely on such disturbances for their illusion of motion.

When you stare at the paintings, they seem to spring to life. Afterimages of the black and white rays (below) overlap to create a pattern called moiré (maw-RAY). The moiré seems to fan out across the rays. What's more, a mysterious energy field seems to be shimmering above the surface of the painting. The activity appears irregular, jittery.

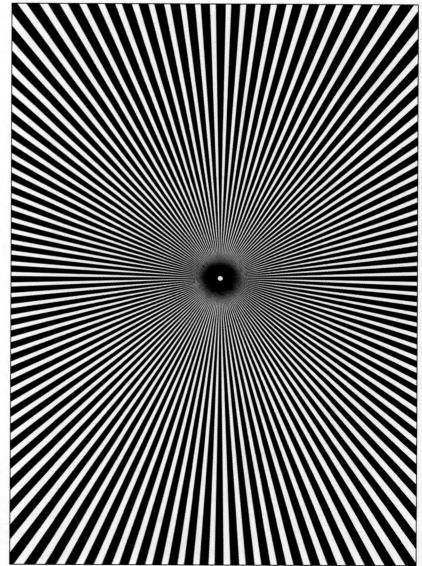

Motion pictures: Stand back and stare at "Shimmer" (right) for a few seconds and you'll sense agitation—disorganized activity—in the painting. A shifting pattern called moiré appears, disappears, and reappears in another place. A swarm of energy particles seems to shimmer above the rays. When the center is blocked and rings are added (left), the agitation disappears, and the activity shifts to the rings. Shadows appear to race around inside them. French artist Isia Leviant created both paintings. The one with the rings has the name "Enigma." The word means "mystery"—and scientists are mystified as to why the rings do what they do.

ISIA LEVIANT (BOTH)

11

French artist Isia Leviant discovered something curious when he added rings and a central disk to the rays (page 10). The rings seemed to capture and tame the activity. With the additions, Leviant succeeded in creating organized, continuous motion. Scientists can't yet explain what brings about this change from uncontrolled activity to controlled movement.

You see illusions of one kind or another every day. But you don't think of them as illusions unless you have reason to doubt what you see. For instance, as you look down a long road, its sides appear to draw closer and closer together. They don't, of course, as experience has shown you. Every time you look in a mirror you experience an illusion. You're not *really* behind the looking glass and reversed from left to right, as you well know. When you see a Christmas tree lying

From one viewpoint, the tops of two buildings in Los Angeles, California, seem to be converging **(left)**. *But experience tells you the buildings are only tall, not tilting. A different camera angle* **(above)** *proves it.*

13

on its side, it looks shorter than it will when you stand it up in your living room. The tree hasn't changed; your perception of it has.

You'd see size illusions all the time if it weren't for something called *size scaling*. This is the remarkable ability of the brain to adjust the size information that comes from the retinal image. It enables you to see an object as being of constant size *in spite of changes in its distance*. An experiment shows size scaling at work.

Hold your left hand in front of you at arm's length. Hold your right hand at half the distance. Both hands look about the same size, right? In fact, the retinal image of the near hand is *twice* as high and wide as the image of the far hand. The brain overrides this size clue. You see the hands as being of about equal size—which, of course, they are.

Now, get an idea of what your world would look like without size scaling. Hold your hands as before, *(Continued on page 18)*

△ Visiting the White House?
A guard stands duty at the door,
meaning the President is in. But
wait—things aren't exactly what they
seem. The "clue" is Joe Armstrong,
6, of Lancaster, Pennsylvania. He
puts the mansion in proper scale.

◁ Even the pictures are picture-
perfect inside the Red Room. The
hand, however, gives its size away.
Florida artists John and Jan Zweifel
built the White House model.

15

On a windy winter night, your imagination can play tricks on you. It can cause you to see all sorts of illusions. You may see faces in the blowing curtains. Objects caught in the moonlight cast spooky shadows on the walls. Happily, it's easy to get rid of these eerie images. Just turn on the lights!

BARBARA L. GIBSON

16

(Continued from page 14) with one near, one far. Move the near hand so that it partly covers the other hand. Overlapping defeats the process of size scaling. Now the near hand *does* look much larger.

Size scaling helps you make sense of the things around you. It helps prevent objects from appearing to shrink or grow alarmingly as their distance from you changes. Without size scaling, your world would seem strange, even frightening. An experiment done several years ago shows how this could be.

A certain African tribe lived in the thick forest. Scientists brought members of the tribe to a plain, something they had never seen before. Shown buffalo in the distance, they mistook them for insects nearby. When the buffalo moved closer, the tribespeople thought the "insects" were growing bigger and bigger. They became frightened.

Accustomed to the forest, the tribespeople had no experience with distance beyond a few yards. They had never had a need to develop fully the size-scaling ability.

Your brain is always trying to come up with its best guess about what your eyes take in. Sometimes, though, it can't quite decide what the best bet is. The painting at right pops in and out of shape before your eyes as the brain tries to decide which is the "correct" shape. The figures below, though reasonable at a glance, are quite impossible. Yet they resemble *possible* objects so closely that the brain keeps trying to make sense of them.

Illusions like these can be strictly for fun. In the next chapter, you'll discover other tricks artists use to startle or to please the senses. Later, you'll learn how other people use illusions in their work. And you'll get a fresh look at illusions in nature.

All in all, you'll find that when it comes to seeing, there's more than meets the eye.

Want to drive a friend crazy? Challenge your friend to build the shapes printed on the stamps above—or to arrange a bunch of cubes into the shape on the next page. They're impossible figures. Sections of the stamp figures join where they could never meet if they really existed. *Swedish artist Oscar Reutersvärd drew them on flat surfaces, where he could commit some visual mischief. Give it time and the cube figure (right), by French artist Victor Vasarely, will pop in and out. Your brain is "changing its mind" about what it sees.*

18

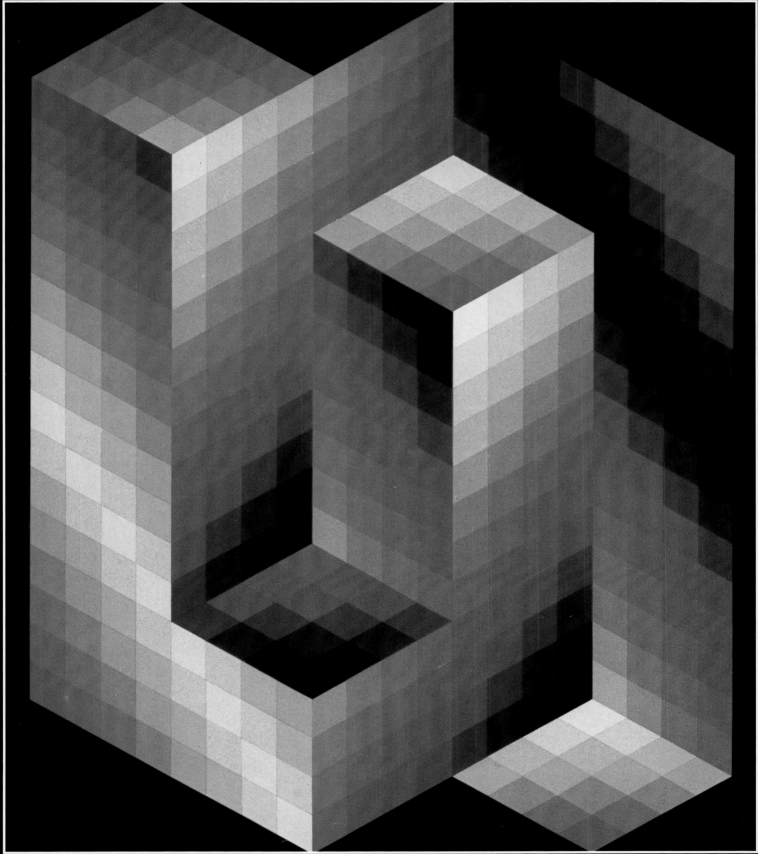

The Artist's Secret Tools

If you're convinced these girls have just come through a mountain underpass, you've been fooled. The only tunnel here was painted on a brick wall by a skillful artist. The girls—from the left, Fredena Williams, 14, Karen Hershberger, 12, and Mariah Maclachlan, 13, all of Columbia, South Carolina—are actually romping in a parking lot beside a bank building. The artist painted the mural in a style called trompe l'oeil (trawmp LOY). It's a French term that means "to deceive the eye." In one way or another, just about all artwork uses visual illusion. You'll find more eye-opening examples on the pages that follow.

MURAL BY BLUE SKY/NATIONAL GEOGRAPHIC PHOTOGRAPHER BRUCE A. DALE

"Everybody is fascinated by the fact that an artist can make something appear to be where it doesn't exist at all," says a painter named Blue Sky. Blue Sky created the mural "Tunnelvision" on pages 20–21. "The mural shows how powerful the imagination can be," he says. "Anything that can show the power of mind over matter is a very pleasant experience. It's magical."

Artists have been using that "magic" for tens of thousands of years—ever since early humans began painting cave walls with animal likenesses. Very possibly those early artists created their paintings as part of magical hunting rituals. They may have believed that drawing the animals helped bring strength and success to the hunter.

Many cave artists made their paintings very realistic. The kinds of animals they painted became extinct long before modern times. But the artwork gives people today a clear idea of how the creatures actually looked those thousands of years ago.

Realism is something that cave art has in common with Blue Sky's work. "When you look at reality, it seems solid," says Blue Sky. "But murals show that you can blast through solid stone to the sky on the other side."

He doesn't mean that you can *actually* blast through stone by making a painting on a wall. But an artist can make an ordinary wall look like something completely different— such as an elegant rotunda (opposite page), or a 1930s movie theater (below). Other artists do the same thing with a piece of canvas.

◁ *Stairway to nowhere: Artist Richard Haas has transformed a brick wall in Cincinnati, Ohio, with the power of paint. The fancy stairway, the domed chamber, the Roman statue—they're all illusions. Haas has created murals in many cities. Some are so realistic that spectators pass by without giving them a second look.*

▷ *Only the cars are real in this scene of a 1930s-style movie house. Haas painted this mural on the side of a building in Homewood, Illinois. He is a master of perspective—the technique that gives the illusion of depth. Notice the shading and the lines formed by the lights under the marquee. After he designs his murals, Haas hires sign painters to complete them.*

MURAL BY RICHARD HAAS/PETER MAUSS (BOTH)

23

◁ In "The Circus," modern folk artist Albina Felski has chosen not to use perspective. As a result, all the action appears to take place at about the same distance. Avoiding the use of depth clues helps give this particular painting a lively, bustling, circuslike effect.

▷ Here's what a similar circus scene looks like with perspective added. You can easily tell at what distance each bit of action is taking place. Figures toward the front are larger and clearer than those in the back. Faces and clothing have more detail. Notice the top and sides of the lion cage. The lines that represent them converge toward a single vanishing point somewhere in the distance.

BARBARA L. GIBSON

A rt enables you to see the world through another person's eyes. When you look at a painting, it's as if you had crawled inside the artist's head. You are free to agree or disagree with the artist's view. You may find the painting beautiful . . . or enraging . . . or inspiring . . . or puzzling . . . or even ugly. Your reaction is up to you. But whatever it is, the art has given you something that you can keep for life: a new way of looking at your world.

Artists create depth and texture where they do not really exist. Artists suggest motion with lines that remain still. They create a variety of colors where no such colors exist. To achieve the illusions they desire, artists make use of many techniques.

You've probably seen paintings in which the scene appears entirely flat. In fact, you probably drew similar pictures yourself when you were younger. The sun, a cloud, a house, the grass, some trees, and you and a pet dog—all appeared at the same distance.

Such paintings lack *perspective*. Artists use perspective to give pictures the illusion of depth. The painter of the circus scene on the opposite page did not use perspective; omitting it gives the painting a more circuslike effect. The scene above is similar to the folk painting, but with the addition of perspective.

In the version with perspective, the artist has made the faces in the distant crowd smaller than the closeup faces of the circus performers. She has made the lines in the foreground thicker and sharper, and those in the background lighter. Shading of the ringmaster's coat and other objects in the foreground suggests texture (Continued on page 29)

25

GEORGES SEURAT, "SUNDAY AFTERNOON ON THE ISLAND OF LA GRANDE JATTE," 1884–86, OIL ON CANVAS, 207.6 x 308 cm; HELEN BIRCH BARTLETT MEMORIAL COLLECTION, 1926.224. (BOTH).

◁ Dots of color—hundreds of thousands of dots—make up this painting of an afternoon in the park. French painter Georges Seurat created it. Seurat, who died in 1891 at age 32, devoted his brief career to experimenting with color and light. He used dots, rather than brushstrokes or lines, to represent objects. Instead of mixing his colors on the canvas, Seurat let the viewer's eye-brain do the blending. This well-known painting, "Sunday Afternoon on the Island of La Grande Jatte," measures 10 feet (3 m)* across. Seurat spent two years working on it.

△ Detail of figures in "La Grande Jatte" shows how the dots work together to produce color, light, and shadow. Seurat was one of the Impressionists—artists who painted their impressions of a moment in time. The dots earned Seurat's style the name Pointillism.

27

*Metric figures in this book have been rounded off.

Dots make the shot: Seurat was on to something when he used tiny dots to build colored images on canvas. Modern printing presses reproduce photographs in much the same way. Patterns of dots of only four basic colors are printed on white paper. The colors are red, yellow, blue, and black. In various combinations, they make up all the possible colors. The detail above shows the pattern of dots in the face of the boy at right. The eye-brain combines all the dots and sees the picture as a whole.

NATIONAL GEOGRAPHIC PHOTOGRAPHER JAMES P. BLAIR (BOTH)

28

(*Continued from page 25*) and form—detail that gives the impression of nearness.

Depth can also be shown with converging lines. Look at a tabletop from a position in front of and a little above it. You'll see that the sides appear to converge. In the circus painting with perspective, the artist has made the sides of the lion cage converge. Artists have a term for the point at which the converging lines would meet if extended long enough. They call it the "vanishing point."

Artists, of course, have many ways of showing motion and activity. Suppose you were an artist capturing the motion of a girl running. How would you go about it?

First, you'd catch her in midstride. That way, the viewer will see the immediate action and *imagine* what it was a moment before and a moment after. Next, you might show the girl's hair streaming behind her. Her motion is so swift that it's creating its own breeze! Then, as a finishing touch, you might paint a shadow below her raised foot. The shadow will emphasize that the girl is above the ground, springing through the air.

Artists may fool your eyes with color, too. The modern British painter Bridget Riley has made nearly a lifelong study of color. As a child, she would gaze at the seascapes near her home. She'd watch how the ocean changed color as the light changed. She'd notice how the sun splashed light against rocks and cliffs. She'd wonder at the light and shadows in footprints in the sand.

Bridget Riley paints in a style called op, or optical, art. Two of her works appear on the next pages. At first glance, they may look like little more than soothing, colorful patterns. But there's more to them than that. When you back off and let your gaze linger,

△ *Good ol' Charlie Brown. What would we do without his annual football misadventure? Cartoonist Charles Schulz uses a number of devices to show the action. "Speed lines" streak behind Charlie in panels 5 and 6. They indicate motion. Quick pen strokes around Charlie in panel 7 suggest bouncing. A bold-lettered "WHAM!" with more speed lines shows the force of his fall. The star and looping line in panel 8 indicate dizziness. Schulz uses these devices without giving them much thought. "I just let the pen go where it will go," he says.*

29

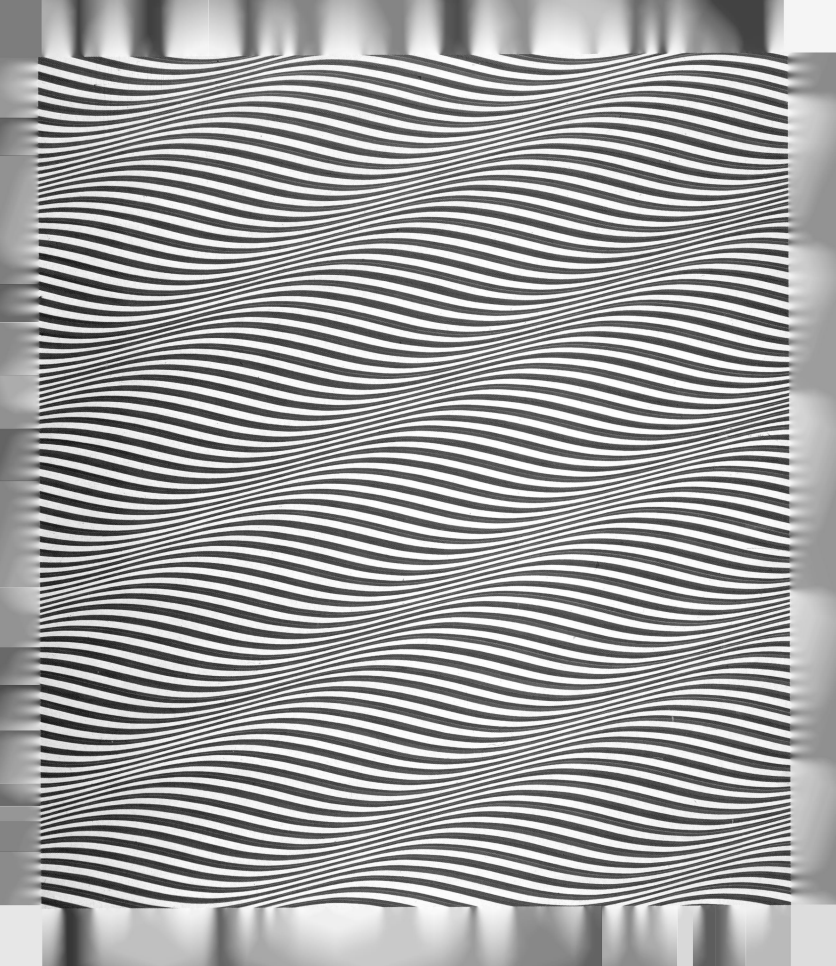

◁ *You can almost reach out and feel the gently rolling texture of this painting. It's "Gala," by British artist Bridget Riley. Depth isn't the only illusion that she has created here. After stepping back and gazing at the painting for a while, you may begin to see yellow and pink and lavender. Those colors do not exist in the art. "Gala," by the way, means "joyous celebration."*

▷ *Another Bridget Riley painting shimmers and ripples with colors that might remind you of a tropical fish or of a peacock's tail. There's actually a lot of white in both paintings, though you have to look close to see it. The brain fills in the white strips with color. Riley says she gets her inspiration from colors she saw in nature as a child.*

"GALA" AND "CLEPSYDRA" COURTESY JUDA ROWAN GALLERY

the paintings begin to do odd things. Movement appears where there is none. You see colors that do not exist on the canvas.

"I work from nature," says the artist, "but in completely new terms. For me, nature is not a landscape, but a visual event."

Bridget Riley—and many other artists—have also found inspiration in a group of painters called Impressionists. Op art is not at all like Impressionism. But Riley has long admired the way the Impressionists used color.

The Impressionists got their start in France in the 1860s. They were fascinated by the way light fell on objects. As a result, their paintings dazzled the eye with light and color.

For years, detailed realism had been the goal of artists. The new painters wanted instead to create *impressions* of what they saw. They wanted to capture an instant in time. That instant might be a moment of bright sunlight. It might be a mood, a feeling.

To help capture that special instant, Impressionists tried new ways of applying paint. Early Impressionists used dabs and dabs of color to build the surfaces of their canvases. Some later Impressionists, such as Georges Seurat (rhymes with "hurrah"), used tiny dots of color to create their scenes. You can see his most famous painting, of Parisians on a Sunday outing, on pages 26–27.

People at first were shocked by the new, relaxed style. It was the work of "cross-eyed minds," hissed one critic. "Unheard-of, appalling," scoffed another. A third critic found the style "awful, stupid, dirty," and felt it "had no common sense." Still another noted how one "poor soul," after viewing an Impressionist exhibit, "was arrested in the street . . . [for] biting the passers-by."

But Impressionism caught on. People became more aware of *how* a work was painted. Now they would ask: What kind of brushwork did the painter use? How does the technique add to the painting's effect?

31

What tricks does the artist play with light and color? What mood does the artist create?

It was a new way of looking at art.

When you look at the vase at left, you see one of two things. You either see a vase . . . or you see silhouettes of Elizabeth II, Queen of England, and her husband, Prince Philip. As the images shift back and forth, the dark area becomes either negative space (background) or positive space (object).

One 20th-century artist was particularly fascinated by the relationship between positive and negative space. The artist was M. C. Escher, a printmaker from Holland. "Our eyes," wrote Escher, "are accustomed to fixing on a specific object. The moment this happens, everything [around the object] becomes reduced to background."

Escher used that knowledge in many of his works. He combined it with a belief that "the passage of time . . . can be suggested by the repetition and change of similar shapes." In "Sky and Water I" (below), a flight of birds changes into a school of fish. Background becomes object. But which is the background— the light area or the dark? And where does it begin and end?

Escher also delighted (Continued on page 37)

◁ *Vase . . . or faces? It depends on whether you focus on the background or the object. The object (positive space) is a vase. The background (negative space) forms silhouettes of a well-known royal couple.*

▽ *Negative and positive space make up the emblem of the Girl Scouts of the U.S.A. The outline of the emblem is the familiar trefoil shape seen on Girl Scout badges, pins, and cookies. The faces alternate, white on black, black on white. One face becomes background for the next, which in turn becomes background for the next. The contrasting black and white profiles symbolize the membership, which includes Scouts of all ethnic groups.*

GIRL SCOUTS OF THE U.S.A.

GIRL SCOUTS

△ *Subject becomes background, and background becomes subject in "Sky and Water I." It's a woodcut by Dutch artist M. C. Escher. To Escher, negative shapes and positive shapes were equally important. Can you see the swimming fish at the same instant you see the flying birds? Most people find it impossible!*

33

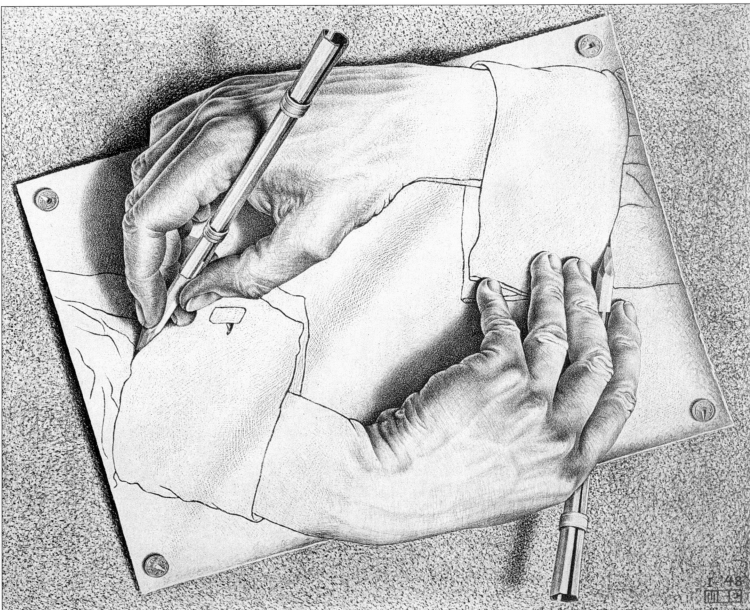

△ You've got to hand it to Escher: He knew how to create an illusion. In "Drawing Hands," two hands appear to pop right off a piece of paper—as they draw each other's shirt cuffs. You could spend a lifetime trying to figure out which hand began the drawing, and you'd never come up with the answer.

▷ At first glance, everything appears in order in "Waterfall." The water mill from long ago looks like a great place to explore. But wait—a close second look shows that things are terribly amiss. Some of the columns that support the water trough are placed in impossible positions. Then there's the water: While flowing down the stepped trough, it's actually headed uphill! Escher, who lived from 1898 to 1972, delighted in teasing people with his art. Many of his illusions use complicated mathematical principles. Yet Escher, as he himself put it, "never got a passing grade in math."

34

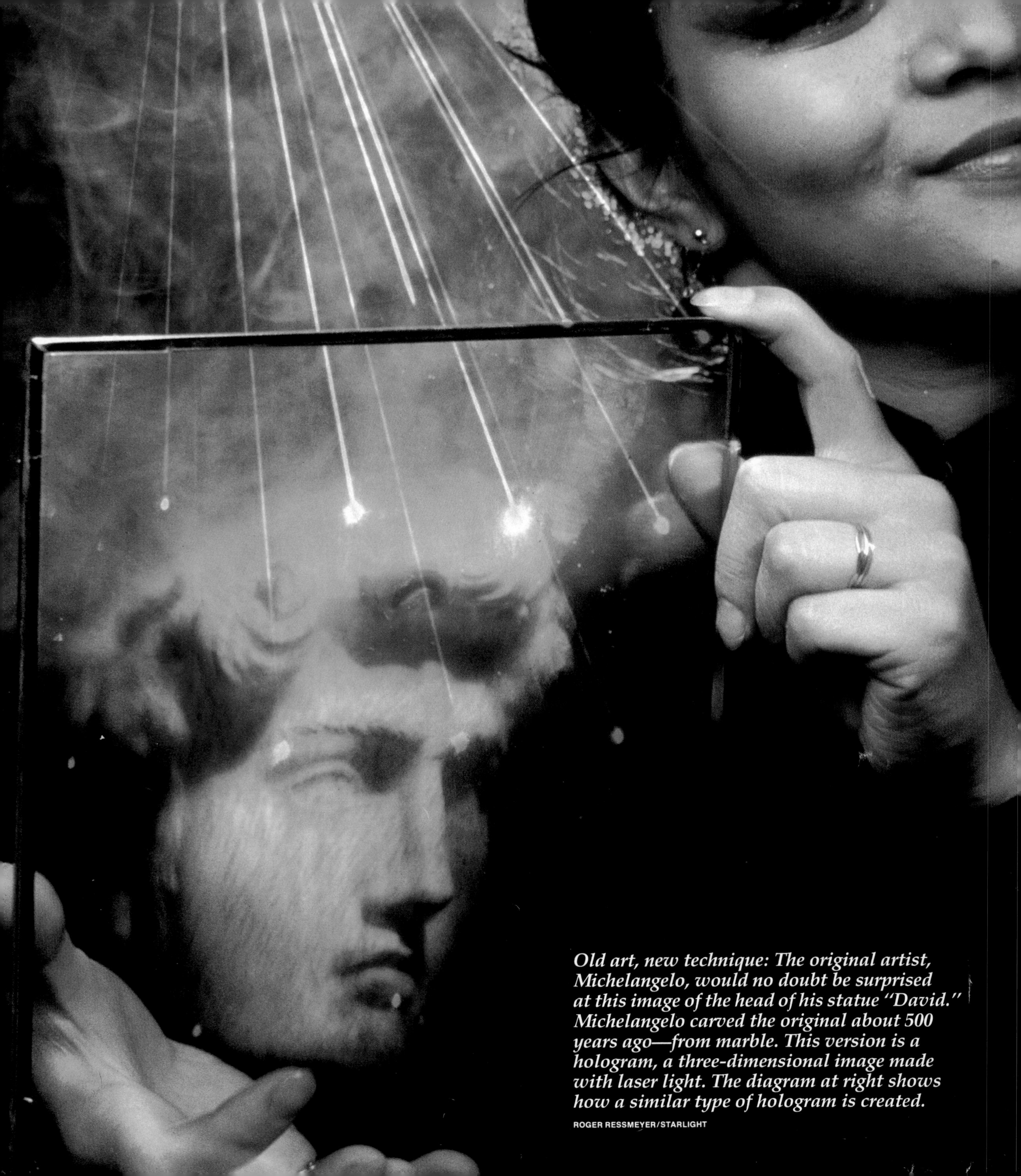

Old art, new technique: The original artist, Michelangelo, would no doubt be surprised at this image of the head of his statue "David." Michelangelo carved the original about 500 years ago—from marble. This version is a hologram, a three-dimensional image made with laser light. The diagram at right shows how a similar type of hologram is created.

ROGER RESSMEYER/STARLIGHT

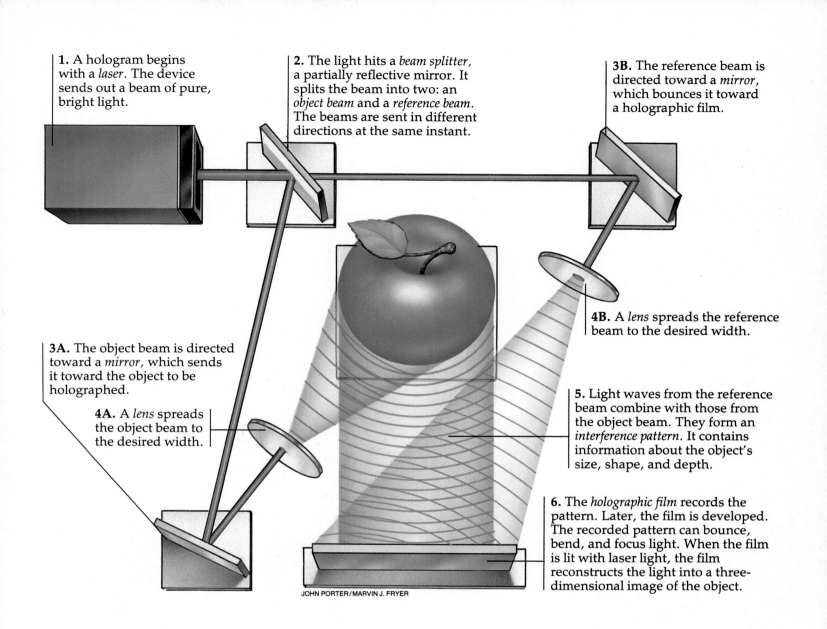

1. A hologram begins with a *laser*. The device sends out a beam of pure, bright light.

2. The light hits a *beam splitter*, a partially reflective mirror. It splits the beam into two: an *object beam* and a *reference beam*. The beams are sent in different directions at the same instant.

3B. The reference beam is directed toward a *mirror*, which bounces it toward a holographic film.

4B. A *lens* spreads the reference beam to the desired width.

3A. The object beam is directed toward a *mirror*, which sends it toward the object to be holographed.

4A. A *lens* spreads the object beam to the desired width.

5. Light waves from the reference beam combine with those from the object beam. They form an *interference pattern*. It contains information about the object's size, shape, and depth.

6. The *holographic film* records the pattern. Later, the film is developed. The recorded pattern can bounce, bend, and focus light. When the film is lit with laser light, the film reconstructs the light into a three-dimensional image of the object.

JOHN PORTER/MARVIN J. FRYER

(*Continued from page 33*) in creating scenes that defied the laws of physics. Look at "Waterfall" on page 35. Everything seems normal, doesn't it? Now take a close look at the course of the water. The water flows *downward* from the foot of the fall. But it ends up mysteriously *feeding the fall at the top!*

It's an impossible situation. Water can't flow uphill—yet here it does. "Waterfall" is convincing at the same time it's baffling. By looking, you'll find more surprises in the work. "I am out to give people a shock," Escher once said. He succeeded.

ow art has entered the age of high technology. Using laser light rather than brushes and paint, a new type of artist creates a new type of art (opposite page). It's the hologram, a special kind of three-dimensional image. Many kinds of holograms make you think you are seeing an object. What you're actually seeing is recorded light patterns.

Only laser light can make a hologram. Ordinary light is made up of waves of different lengths. They scatter in all directions. The waves that make up laser light are all of

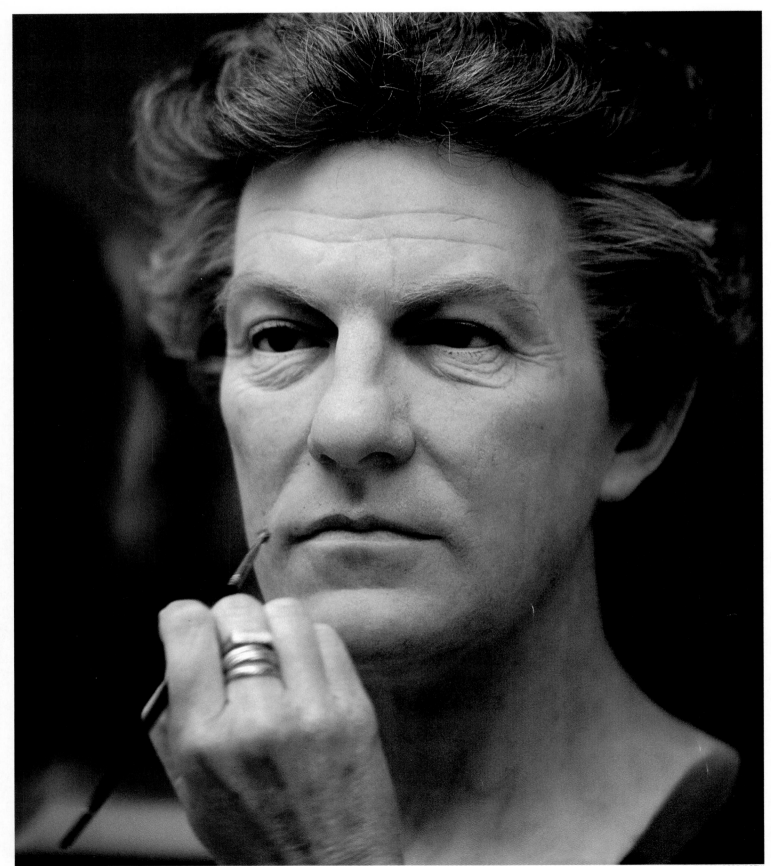

the same length. They move in unison, like a well-drilled marching band.

It's this quality of laser light that's important in making holograms. Laser-light patterns are orderly and predictable. They can be recorded and reproduced as a clear image. Ordinary light would produce merely a colorful blur.

The cave artists could never have imagined such a thing as a hologram. But if a cave artist and a high-tech artist could meet, they'd probably understand each other's views about such things in art as color and depth and motion. And if you were to view a cave painting together with a sample of modern art, one piece might affect you in much the same way as the other. "The aim of art," wrote Aristotle, a wise man of ancient Greece, "is to represent not the outward appearance of things, but their inward significance."

◁ *Now, don't move! Actually, the makeup artist doesn't have to worry that her model will wiggle as she applies the paint. The model is wax. A sculptor created the figure for Madame Tussaud's, a wax museum in London, England. The artist worked from photographs and precise measurements of the subject, British photographer Lord Patrick Lichfield.*

△ *Seeing double: The real Lord Lichfield, on the left, leans on his wax twin. Did you think the figure on the right was the real Lord Lichfield? It's hard to tell the difference. The photographer and the wax figure wear identical outfits—right down to their expensive cameras. Madame Tussaud's has been displaying wax doubles of famous people since 1835.*

39

3

Putting Illusions to Work

Like giant animals, armored vehicles called Imperial Walkers lumber across an icebound planet during a battle scene in the movie *The Empire Strikes Back*. The walkers look huge, but they're really only knee-high models. The landscape seems authentic, but the snow is actually baking soda, and the sky and hills are a painted backdrop. Miniature sets like this one help produce exciting scenes in just about every movie you see. Special effects experts create them. But illusion doesn't belong to the movie industry alone. Professionals in other fields also put visual tricks to work. Some of the jobs illusions do will surprise you.

△ Secret of the Imperial Walkers: Special effects expert Jon Berg pops his head through a trapdoor to adjust an Imperial Walker during the filming of The Empire Strikes Back. After each frame of film was shot, Berg changed the model's position by a fraction of an inch. Then the cameraman shot another frame. The technique is called stop motion. When the completed scene is projected, the model will seem to move smoothly and naturally.

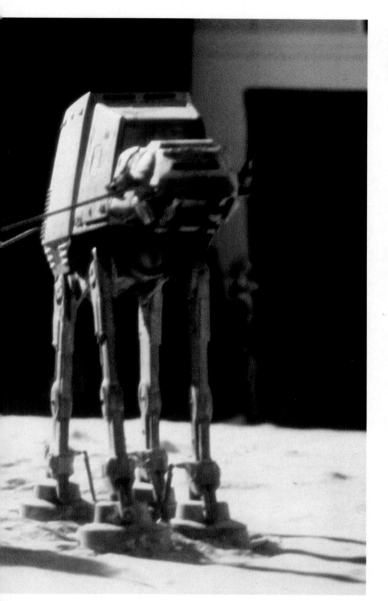

<At a studio in northern California, Empire technicians arrange a set for the ice planet Hoth. Stop-motion scenes of Imperial Walkers launching an attack were filmed here. At the same time, far away in Norway, filmmakers shot scenes of actors on a real glacier. Later, in a special optical device, the scenes of the actors and of the miniatures were combined. When moviegoers watched the final product, they experienced the illusion of a dramatic battle between people and machines on a strange, snowy planet.

In a darkened theater, a seated audience stares at the action on the screen. Spaceships whiz around mysterious planets; spectacular battles take place; huge metal monsters march across a frozen landscape.

The movie is *The Empire Strikes Back*. Set in deep space, *Empire* spins out the saga of a war between the forces of good and evil. Large parts of the movie consist of special effects—pure illusion. Moviegoers may *know* that the story unfolding before them is a fantasy, filmed mostly in a California studio. But the special effects *are* convincing. The audience is willing to be taken in for a while and to believe the action is really taking place.

Actually, you could say that every movie consists entirely of illusion. For one thing, the image doesn't really move. For another, the viewer is staring at a blank screen for half the movie's running time.

Still images called frames make up every motion picture. Each second, 24 slightly different frames flicker across the screen. Between frames, a shutter blocks the projector light, and the screen turns black. One period of darkness lasts about as long as one flash of a frame. You don't notice the blank screen at all, however. Your eye-brain fills in the dark gaps with afterimages. You see a constantly bright, continuously moving image.

The illusion is a powerful one, and an entire industry has grown up around it. That industry, motion pictures, has in turn brought into being or helped develop dozens of entertainment-related professions—one of which deals with special effects.

In motion pictures, a special effect is an illusion produced by mechanical or optical devices. One special effect you see all the time is the fade-out/fade-in. The screen fades from full exposure to blackness, then fades back to full exposure. Only a few seconds have actually gone by—but the illusion is one of a long passage of time.

43

△ Dressed in his finest, Captain EO and other characters burst from the screen. That's how moviegoers see this scene from the 3–D science fantasy Captain EO. Michael Jackson plays the title role, using the power of dance and music to win over opposing forces. Captain EO was produced for the Walt Disney Company's theme parks.

▷ An audience at Walt Disney World Epcot Center, near Orlando, Florida, wears special glasses to enjoy the 3–D action in Captain EO. Without the glasses, the audience would see a blur of overlapping images.

44

You've no doubt watched movie scenes in which a car crashes through the wall of a building. Bricks fly and tumble everywhere. If you guessed that the "bricks" were actually Styrofoam, light and harmless as feathers, you were right.

Not all special effects are so simple to achieve. They may require special equipment. Many 3–D movies, for example, are shot with a pair of cameras and screened with two projectors (below).

In addition to equipment, many special effects require elaborate planning and exact timing. If everything is done perfectly, you believe the effect. If not, you're likely to notice and say, "Aw, that's just a fake!"

It's unlikely you'll make the comment about *Empire* and other Star Wars movies. The producers did make frequent use of miniatures, but on screen they looked real. Finicky detail helped make the models believable. For example, craftsmen etched more than 250,000 portholes into the Star Destroyer *Executor*. Neon tubing, designed to give just the right glow, lighted the ship from within. This model alone cost $100,000. It took 14 people 7 weeks to build.

All together, nearly 400 models appeared in the Star Wars films. The Death Star, a space city, looked on-screen to be the size of a small planet. In reality it measured only $3\frac{1}{2}$ feet (1 m) in diameter. Models of some craft came in different sizes. One version of the Y-wing fighter would fit in a teacup.

Empire featured fast-paced battle scenes showing many spacecraft in action at once. Actually, the movement of each craft was shot separately. Technicians eliminated

Three-D movies work by giving you two slightly different images. Your brain combines them into one image that has depth. Two cameras were used to film Captain EO. *One takes in light from the right-eye viewing angle; the other, from the left.*

*Two projectors cast the filmed image onto a metallic screen (**right, top**). The projected light consists of vibrating waves. Each projector has a filter that polarizes, or lines up, its light waves. One filter lines them up vertically; the other aligns them horizontally.*

*The two polarized images bounce off the screen toward the viewers (**right, bottom**). A second set of filters, the 3–D glasses, ensures that the right eye receives only the right-eye view, the left eye only the left. The brain combines the two images to create one that has depth.*

JOHN PORTER/STEVE WAGNER

unwanted image from each set of shots—ceilings, studio lights, stage floors. The shots were then combined into one shot in a device called an optical printer. The resulting film showed all the craft "acting" together, swerving and diving and zooming and firing.

When a miniature spaceship explodes, the event isn't spectacular at all. The explosion lasts only half a second or so. The blast sounds hardly as loud as a firecracker pop. Special effects crews make the explosion seem huge. The scene is shot at the rate of 240 frames a second. When projected at 24 frames a second, the explosion lasts a full 5 seconds. Added sound sharpens the drama.

Many movie landscapes you'd swear were real are paintings on a pane of glass. Where the director wants action to appear, an area is left clear. A piece of frosted plastic is placed behind it. Next, a filmed action scene is projected onto the plastic from behind. A camera in front of the painting films the complete scene. Any telltale "rough edges" are blended optically. In *Return of the Jedi*, the Ewok village is a glass painting. So is the huge warehouse at the end of *Raiders of the Lost Ark*.

◁ *Lost in space? No — caught in a trick photograph. Michel Tcherevkoff created this picture for the cover of a national magazine. Using simple materials, he made the picture in his photographic studio in New York City.*

MICHEL TCHEREVKOFF (LEFT)

▽ *Using wires, Tcherevkoff positioned colored Ping-Pong balls around the model's head. A Plexiglas sheet covered with more balls forms the base of the image. Above the model's head hangs a plastic planet.*

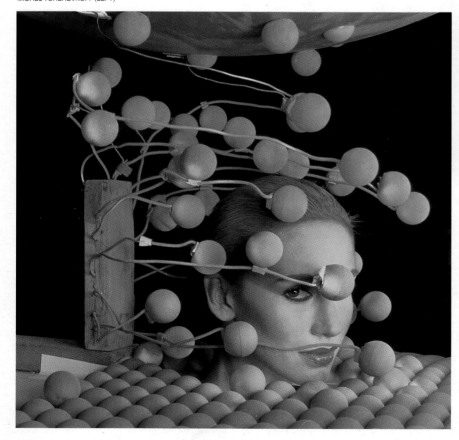

△ *Tcherevkoff makes final adjustments in the arrangement of the "floating" balls. Positioning the balls took hours, for visible wires would have given the trick away. "I plan everything in my mind beforehand," says Tcherevkoff. "But it can always change after I look through the camera's viewfinder. For me, that's the magic of photography."*

© ELIZABETH HATHON (BOTH)

Special effects people have hundreds of tricks up their sleeves. Now you know how they accomplish some of the major ones. The experts try to make sure their tricks can't be detected. After all, being fooled is at least half the fun of going to the movies!

Like moviemakers, still photographers often deal in illusion. Photographers like their pictures to tell a story or to show a mood. Sometimes that's a matter of luck—capturing the subject at just the right moment. The pictures on these pages show such lucky catches. To make pictures like these, you'll need a quick shutter finger and an imaginative eye.

Usually a trick shot has to be set up—and that can be a time-consuming task. To create the mood-making picture on page 46, the photographer had to paint nearly a thousand Ping-Pong balls. After that, he had to position them just so. The photograph, showing a model in a dreamlike world, made the cover of *American Photographer* magazine.

Advertisements in magazines make heavy use of illusion. Advertising is big business, and advertisers want to make sure their messages grab people's attention. Illusions often help do that better than ordinary shots.

The law prohibits advertisers from using fakes for an item actually being sold. Ad directors may, however, use props for other items that appear in the ad. Food photographer Dick Frank, (Continued on page 53)

△ *Strange beast: A six-legged, two-horned rhinoceros trots across an African plain—or so it appears. Actually, the photographer caught two rhinos at just the right instant, making them look like a single, very unusual creature.*

▷ *High view, low view—an ostrich seems to have the scene covered. Of course, it's another trick photograph. Only the neck and head of a second bird are visible behind the body of the first. You too can make pictures like these—but you've got to be fast. Says photographer Nicholas DeVore III, who made this picture: "I got only one frame before the ostriches moved."*

48

◁ To get close-ups of animals, wildlife photographers sometimes use hideouts called blinds. Here, at a watering hole in Africa, a photographer's assistant hides inside a blind that looks like a termite mound. Unsuspecting, the elephant comes close for a portrait.

△ Camouflaged netting hides photographer Jim Brandenburg as he waits to make pictures of great blue herons in New Mexico. "The idea," he says, "is to break up the human form."

◁ Brandenburg carries his blind—reeds attached to a rubber inner tube. He will use it to photograph waterfowl in a North Dakota marsh. Waiting for the birds, Brandenburg will stand waist deep in water, his head and shoulders hidden behind the blind. Wading pants will help keep him dry.

51

(Continued from page 48)   of New York City, describes some tricks of the trade:

"The ice cubes in a soft-drink ad are usually hand-carved Plexiglas. Real ice melts under studio lights. It also shifts more readily, and that makes focusing difficult.

"When ice cream appears as a prop, it may actually be colored shortening. Handled properly, it looks like real ice cream—and it keeps its shape. What appears to be coffee in an ad may be a watered-down coloring agent for gravy. Real coffee has oils in it that can produce an undesirable rainbow effect."

Look at food and other types of packages. You'll rarely see a package done in dark colors. That's because light-colored objects appear larger than dark-colored objects. The customer thinks he's   (Continued on page 57)

◁ *Wooden decoys float on the Chester River in Maryland. Placed there by a hunter, they look like family groups of geese paddling along. The decoys may fool the real geese, in the sky, into flying closer.*

△ *On an island off the coast of Maine, a puffin, left, stands among decoys placed there by the National Audubon Society, a conservation group. Because of overhunting, puffins vanished in the 1800s from their island homes. Now people are trying to lure them back. The Audubon Society reports that the efforts are working.*

53

▷ Mirror, mirror on the wall . . . Architects used reflective glass for the facade (fuh-SAHD), or outer wall, of this office building in Greenwich, Connecticut. The result: Instead of appearing to be a massive space taker, the building blends in with the sky. Architects use illusion to create a variety of effects.

△ In Dallas, a skyscraper's mirrored facade reflects images of other structures. In addition to presenting an interesting, almost liquid appearance, the reflective glass saves on air-conditioning costs. It bounces the heat of the Texas sun away from the building.

△ *Masterpiece of illusion: On a hill overlooking Athens, Greece, the Parthenon stands great and graceful. The ancient Greeks built the Parthenon between 447 and 438 B.C. People have long admired the structure as an example of architectural perfection. The perfection is based on illusion. Lines that look straight are in fact slightly curved. Columns that seem truly vertical actually lean inward.*

(Continued from page 53) getting more. In new-car ads, notice the ground. It's almost always wet or slick. The reflection gives the scene a look of added luxury.

Photographers, and hunters too, use still another type of illusion. It's a blind. Its purpose is not to trick people but to fool animals into coming close. Decoys—fake birds—may be used to attract waterfowl. Decoys date from the days of ancient Egypt. The impostors are placed on the surface of a pond or a lake to look like birds at rest. Migrating flocks may mistake them for real birds and come in for a landing.

Decoy carving today provides a living for a number of artisans. And demand for fine older models has made auctioneers happy. Just a few years ago, a prized 19th-century goose was sold at auction. The winning bid: twenty-eight thousand dollars!

Decoys have their use mostly in the country. To find illusion on a larger scale, look to the cities. Architects make skyscrapers seem taller than they are by tapering them upward. Mirrored glass can make a building appear to blend in with the sky. By adjusting the lighting, a designer can make a room seem either smaller or larger, whichever is desired.

Many of the tricks used by architects and designers today have (Continued on page 61)

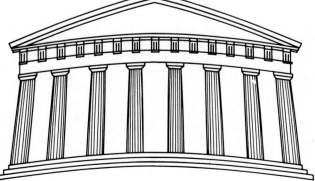

ART: MARVIN J. FRYER

◁ *Without the optical corrections, the Parthenon would look somewhat as it does at far left. The drawing is greatly exaggerated to show the contrast more clearly. Perfectly straight lines would actually have made the Parthenon appear to sag. Truly vertical columns would have seemed to lean outward. As a whole, the Parthenon would have looked weak and humble. The drawing at left, also exaggerated, shows the effect of the architects' corrections. With the adjustments the building looks proud, sound, and upright.*

57

住友館

◁ A gigantic cube seems to float right through the Sumitomo Pavilion in Tsukuba, Japan. The building was designed for Expo '85, a science fair held in Tsukuba. Only part of the cube actually exists; the rest is a reflection bounced back from the pavilion's mirrored facade. The illusion is a powerful one. It's all but impossible to tell where reality ends and reflection begins.

◁ *Shake, rattle, and roll: A flight simulator imitates the sensations of actual flight. It moves so realistically that some trainees become airsick. Pilots train in the simulator to get practical—but safe—experience in handling emergencies. Here, the machine simulates the motion of a plane caught in a violent rush of wind.*

▷ *In the simulator cockpit, trainers John Perkins, left, and Jim Day make a "landing" at Stapleton International Airport, in Denver, Colorado. A computer provides a constantly changing view of the runway.*

ROGER RESSMEYER/STARLIGHT (BOTH)

(Continued from page 57) been known for thousands of years. The ancient Greeks were masters of illusion. You can see that in their famous temple the Parthenon (pages 56–57).

Built in Athens 2,500 years ago, the Parthenon, even in ruins, is impressive. To help make it so, the builders relied on a curious optical fact: A curved line can appear straighter than a straight line!

The major "straight lines" of the Parthenon are not straight at all. They curve. The curving is slight—only about 4 inches in 215 feet. But it results in the illusion of perfect straightness. Without the curving, the building would appear to sag in the middle.

The columns of the Parthenon are not truly vertical. They angle slightly inward. The angling prevents the columns from appearing to lean outward toward the top. The angle is tiny. The columns, if extended upward, would not meet until they rose more than a mile above the base.

Modern materials enable architects to design buildings that seem to open up space rather than fill it. Mirrored glass has become a popular material for exteriors. Mirrored buildings seem lighter and airier than do buildings of brick or stone. That's because they reflect skylight and bounce it onto the street instead of filling the street with shadow.

You can use illusion to change the "feel" of a room. Want your bedroom to look larger? Paint the walls white and use bright overhead lighting. The brightness will "open up" the room, making walls and ceiling seem farther away. Want the room to feel cozier? Darken the walls and light the room with small lamps. A red light bulb will add a feeling of warmth. You can have fun experimenting with lighting of different colors to suit your mood.

aking part in a fire drill at school is serious business. The experience you gain can save your life. The drill is a simulation—an enactment or imitation of the real thing. People in certain professions—pilots, for example—go through drills, too. What they learn can save hundreds of lives in an emergency.

▷ Simulators provide one form of illusion; holograms provide another. Here, pilot Jim Gooden uses a holographic display in the cockpit of a Boeing 727. Information from the jet's instruments is projected by laser onto a clear holographic plate in front of his eyes. Gooden can check on vital data without taking his eyes from the flight path.

CHUCK O'REAR (BOTH)

△ Here's a pilot's-eye view of the holographic display. Sky and runway are clearly visible right through the readings. Display numbers show airspeed at 122 knots (140 mph, or 225 km/h); altitude at 960 feet (293 m); and descent at a rate of 650 feet a minute (198 m/m). Other markings show how level the plane is.

▷ Midair illusion: Scientists at the Massachusetts Institute of Technology, in Cambridge, have perfected a computerized holographic image that is projected into midair. It may eventually aid auto makers in analyzing car designs. Here, graduate student Michael Klug examines a free-floating image of a Chevrolet Camaro.

More and more often, the drills take place in flight simulators. These are computer-controlled environments that have the look and the feel of an actual cockpit. On hydraulic legs, a simulator climbs, turns, descends, vibrates. Computer-generated images enable the pilot to "land" in the major airports of the world. The simulator can also duplicate all kinds of weather conditions. It's all done without the pilot's ever leaving the ground.

Using simulators, pilots learn how to deal with a dangerous condition known as wind shear. Wind shear, a sudden, unexpected change in wind direction and speed, can sweep a plane downward like a feather in a waterfall. When it occurs, a pilot may feel that the plane is out of control. But a pilot caught in wind shear has to react fast—very fast. Lives depend on it.

Reading and classroom training alone may not give a pilot adequate preparation for wind shear. If the pilot has dealt with wind shear in a simulator, there's a greater chance that he or she will react instantly and correctly when the real thing occurs. That means nosing up and throttling to full power.

The sights and sounds and motions in a flight simulator are all realistic but not real. Safety experts say, however, that the payoff *is* real—in lives saved.

△ You could read a 3–D comic book with the glasses Dr. Isabella Karle is wearing. Dr. Karle uses the glasses to "read" the shapes of molecules that appear on the computer monitor. A physical chemist, Dr. Karle works at a laboratory in Washington, D. C. Seeing molecular models in three dimensions helps her predict chemical reactions. That's an important part of her research into developing new drugs for treating disease.

▷ Double image: The picture on Dr. Karle's monitor appears in detail here. Viewed through the glasses, the double lines merge into a single 3–D image. This image represents a chemical found in the soil. It is under study for possible use as an antibiotic—a disease fighter.

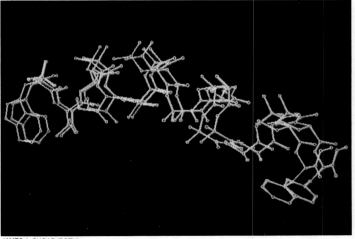

64

JAMES A. SUGAR (BOTH)

three-dimensional images have been around for about 150 years. Until recently, people used them merely for amusement. Today, however, 3–D images have serious uses in science, industry, medicine, and trade.

Many shoppers use 3–D images. The images are holograms that now appear on most major credit cards. The holograms, difficult to forge, give merchants a reasonable assurance that a card is genuine.

Most holograms appear on special foil or coated glass. Now scientists have developed computer-generated holographic images that appear in midair, with nothing between the image and the viewer. "The image is projected into space and floats in front of the observer," says Dr. Stephen A. Benton, of the Massachusetts Institute of Technology, in Cambridge. He invented this type of computer-generated hologram.

The new technique will have wide application. "For example," says Dr. Benton, "architects may use holograms to show clients what a finished building will look like. And auto engineers could evaluate their designs without having to carve clay models."

A few hundred miles south of Cambridge, in Washington, D. C., Dr. Isabella Karle sits at a computer monitor. Her office is cluttered with scientific books and journals. Scraps of paper scribbled with formulas and diagrams litter the desktops. Dr. Karle is examining an image that looks

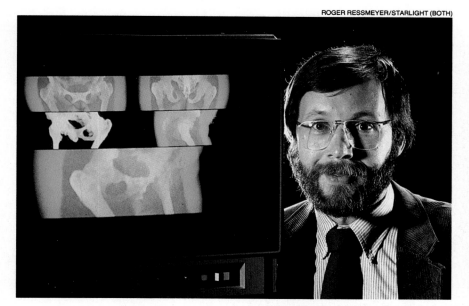

◁ *Hollywood . . . to hospital: The Pixar system, a device invented to produce dramatic special effects in movies, has found a place in surgeons' offices. Edwin A. Catmull of Lucasfilm Ltd. helped invent it. Here, he stands by a Pixar. The machine speeded up the production of action scenes for movies such as* Star Trek II. *It processes picture information at the rate of <u>40 million</u> instructions a second. The device caught the attention of doctors seeking better nonsurgical ways of looking inside the human body.*

▷ *Fed information from computerized X rays, the Pixar system creates three-dimensional views of a body area—here a hip. The image can be rotated so a doctor can see it from any angle. Says the chief surgeon at a leading university hospital: "The Pixar is incredibly exciting. It lets us really visualize what we're trying to repair."*

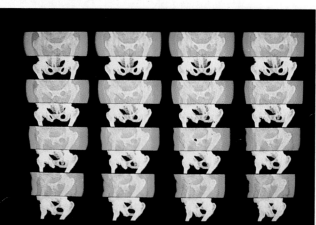

65

something like a colorful Tinkertoy creation. She wears colored glasses much like those provided with a 3–D comic book.

Dr. Karle is a physical chemist with the Naval Research Laboratory. She helps "design" molecules to form new materials.

"The glasses let me see the image in three dimensions," says Dr. Karle. "It's useful to see the cavities formed in a molecule so I can tell what other types of molecules will fit into it and thus create a new compound."

Dr. Karle is working to develop a new antibiotic—medicine that fights certain infectious diseases. She's also helping to develop better chemicals to combat malaria. "Industrially designed molecules may cause fewer side effects than natural ones," she says. "Looking at a 3–D image of a molecule helps us predict possible side effects."

Using 3–D doesn't result in an instantly successful formula. "But," says Dr. Karle, "knowing what the molecule looks like is an important beginning."

Researchers may use illusions to test the subjects of their experiments. For example, the illusion of a steep drop-off (right) was created to test whether a baby at the crawling stage could perceive depth. She could—and so could most other infants tested. The baby crawled along the table but stopped at the drop-off. She continued across the clear glass only after strong reassurances from her mother.

What did the experiment show? It tended to demonstrate that infants may understand more than we give them credit for. Of course, if you've ever seen a baby in action, you've known that all along!

◁ Which way did it go? Scientists sometimes use illusion to help them understand more about vision. Here, subject Greg Lanier can't tell where to reach for a tossed tennis ball. Lanier is wearing prism goggles. The lenses bend light, causing distortion. Could Lanier overcome the visual handicap? That's what the experiment aimed to find out. Lanier did. His eye-brain gradually adjusted. Still wearing goggles, Lanier began catching the ball like a pro.

▷ Only her mother's tender coaxing could persuade this baby to crawl across a "visual cliff." The drop-off is covered by strong, clear glass. Before crossing, the baby hesitated—showing that she had developed the important ability to recognize depth.

NICK KELSH

66

4

When Nature Fools the Eye

To you, the markings on this Rothschildia moth may look like a scary face. But a hungry bird seeing the markings this way would recognize an unexpected treat. Normally, the moth rests hanging from a twig. There its coloring makes it resemble a dead leaf and helps it avoid being noticed by predators. But this moth, attracted to a light during the night, has landed on a healthy leaf. Now its coloration makes the moth easy to spot.

The dead-leaf appearance that normally protects the moth is a form of disguise—one of several kinds of illusions animals use. But natural illusions aren't limited to the animal world. By the end of this chapter, you'll have discovered illusions in the sky, on the ground, and at sea.

I n the animal world, illusion can be a matter of life or death. All but the largest and the fiercest creatures have enemies from which they must protect themselves. Some animals avoid danger by running or flying or jumping away from predators. Others have defenses that enable them to fight off or discourage attackers or any other uninvited guests. Consider the house cat. If a neighborhood dog gets too snoopy, the cat may take a swipe at it with its sharp claws—a good defense.

For many animals, however, the best defense is a good illusion. Animal illusions fall into four main categories: camouflage, mimicry, disguise, and patterns that startle or misdirect.

Look to the left for a remarkable example of camouflage. You might have trouble spotting the fire-bellied toad among the water plants. So might the toad's enemies, because the toad blends in so well with its surroundings. This blending, called camouflage, is perhaps the most common illusion in nature.

Walk through the grass on a summer day. Chances are you'll scare up a number of grasshoppers. You probably won't see them, though, until they spring up just before your foot falls. Their coloring blends in with the grass. If you stand still instead of thrashing through the grass, you might never spot the hoppers at all.

If you take a close look at the creatures in and around a tree in the forest, you'll find many examples of camouflage. The coloration of some moths exactly matches that of tree bark. Resting (Continued on page 74)

◁ *Colored for protection, a fire-bellied toad rests motionless in a duckweed pond. The markings help break up the outline of the toad. The coloring helps the toad blend in with the plants and the water. An enemy would have a hard time spotting the toad. On land, the toad has a second defense. It rises and displays bright orange coloring on its underside. The coloring warns predators that the toad is poisonous.*

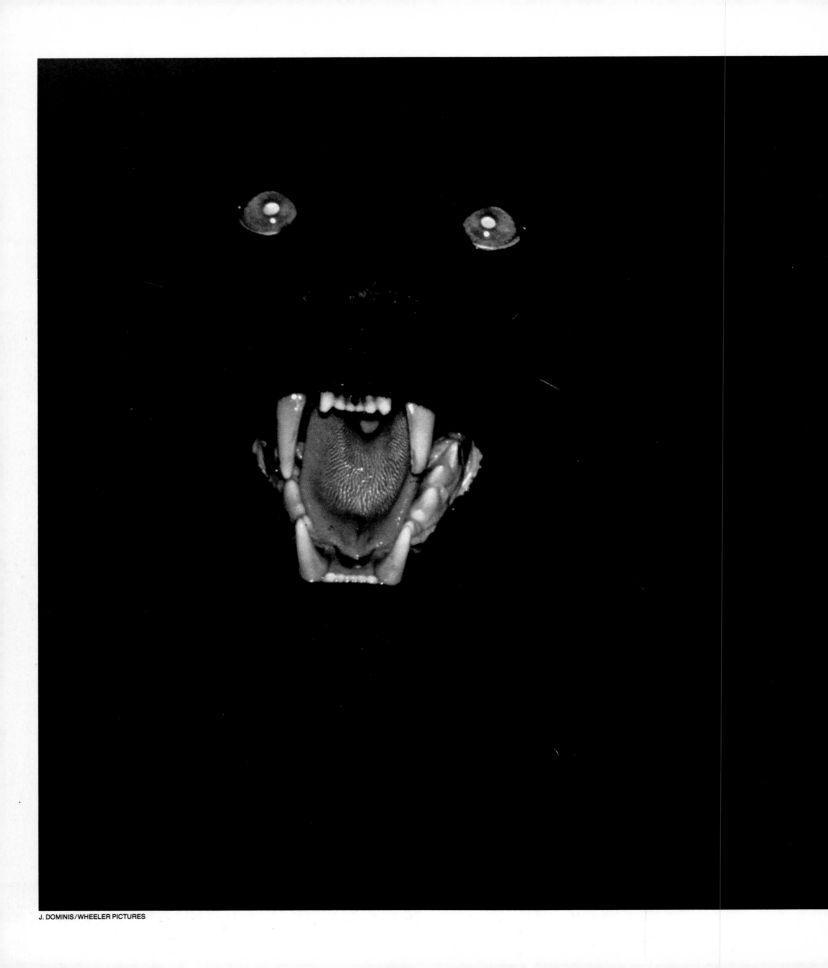

◁ In the dark of night, a black leopard bares its fangs. Only its eyes and gaping mouth can be seen in the photographer's flash. Black leopards are occasionally born among a litter that is of normal color. In the grasslands of Africa, predators easily spot black cubs. Not many survive. But in the dark forests of tropical Asia, the black color helps cubs hide and adults hunt. More black cats survive there.

▽ After a successful hunt, a lioness rests in tall, dry grass. The tawny color of her coat camouflages her. Lions live mostly on the plains of Africa. Females do most of the hunting. They can run swiftly for only short bursts. Camouflage enables them to sneak up close to prey, shortening the chase.

JAMES L. CASTNER

◁ *Animal or vegetable? Even if you look closely, you might miss this leaf insect. It has a disguise that hides it well. It looks like a chewed-on leaf. The insect can stay perfectly still, or it can shake like a leaf in the breeze. Even its eggs are disguised. They look like caterpillar droppings.*

▷ *Hidden hunter: This crab spider's white color hides it from enemies while it waits to ambush a meal. The spider can change color to match a yellow flower, too. To a predator, the red markings may look like the spaces between petals. The crab spider is named for its ability to scurry sideways.*

(*Continued from page 71*) motionless on a tree trunk, the moths avoid detection as birds fly by in search of dinner. Caterpillars feed on leaves that are the same color as they are. The camouflage keeps the caterpillars safe, for the most part. On the ground, a fox pads by. It fails to notice easy prey: a baby bird with wings colored and patterned just like the twigs and dead leaves around its nest.

In the form of illusion known as mimicry, one creature copies the appearance of another creature—one that predators have learned to avoid. The harmless scarlet king snake, for example, has red, black, and yellow markings that mimic those of poisonous coral snakes. An animal that has had a nasty close call with a coral snake will leave both types alone.

To birds, certain monarch butterflies taste bad. Once a bird has gotten sick from one monarch, it leaves all monarchs alone. Another kind of butterfly—the viceroy—benefits from the bad experiences birds have with monarchs. The viceroy looks very much like the monarch. The mimicry is so effective that birds tend to steer clear of it, too. That's too bad for the birds. The viceroy would make a fine meal.

Animals also use disguise. It differs from mimicry in what is being imitated. A disguised animal imitates an *object*, rather than another animal. Predators notice mimicking animals but have learned to avoid them. A predator may notice a disguised animal but not recognize it as something to eat.

Many spiders and insects, for example, disguise themselves as bird droppings. Droppings are unappetizing to predators. Besides, they are so common that they attract little or no attention.

Walk through a woods and you'll probably find some of these imitators. But you must keep a sharp eye out. Their disguises can be remarkably good. A certain type of Central American caterpillar spends its day sitting motionless on a leaf, disguised as a bird dropping. The caterpillar has tiny

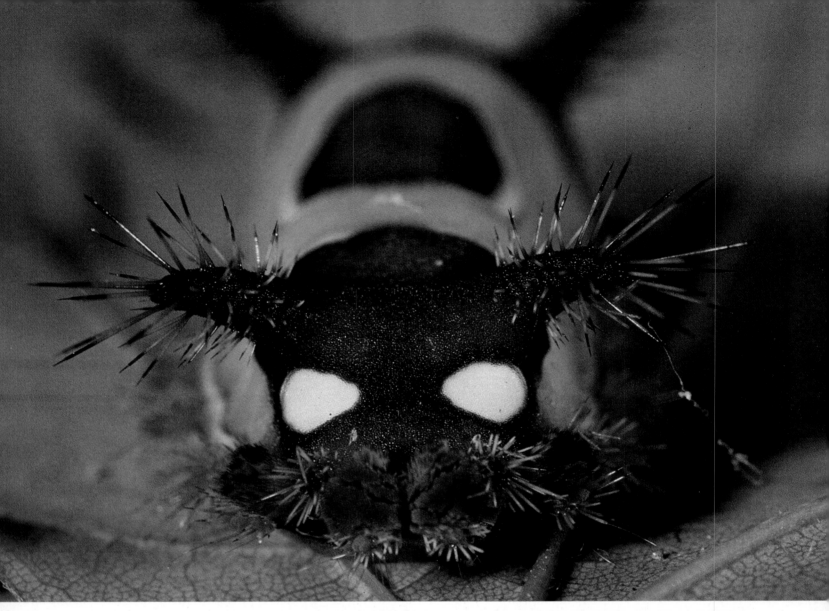

False eyes appear on the tail end of
a saddleback caterpillar *(above)*.
They trick unsuspecting birds into
attacking the wrong end. Instead of
a snack, a bird gets a mouthful of
stinging spines. The caterpillar
escapes serious damage. Such
experiences may teach attackers the
meaning of the bright green saddle
(right): "Warning: I sting!"

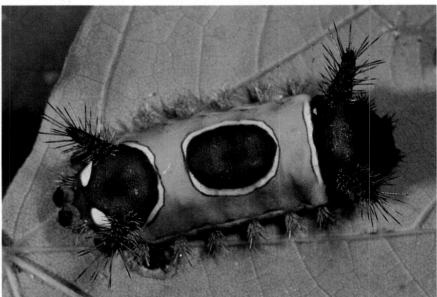

bumps on its skin that look just like berry seeds a bird might have eaten!

Plant parts also attract little attention, and they too are commonly imitated. You could easily mistake the leaf insect on page 74 for a real leaf. Pointy-backed insects called treehoppers look like thorns on a branch. In the tropics alone, some 2,000 kinds of insects disguise themselves as sticks. Some creatures actually create their own disguises. A certain caterpillar on the Asian island of Borneo attaches fresh flower buds to the spines of its body. It replaces them when they wilt.

Illusion works not only to protect prey, but also to help predators. The brownish yellow coat of a lioness (page 73), for example, provides excellent camouflage when she hunts from tall, dry grass.

Some snakes resemble vines. Using this disguise, a snake may sway with the breeze, waiting for a frog or other prey to come along and provide it with a meal. An alligator looks like a floating log—until it snaps its jaws on an unsuspecting bird. To a fish underwater, a sea gull's white (Continued on page 80)

△ Its false head leading the way, a lantern fly walks along a twig. This insect lives in parts of the tropics where alligator relatives called caimans (KAY-munz) swim and crawl. It grows to a length of about 3 inches (8 cm). The false head has markings that resemble a caiman's exposed teeth, bulging eyes, and knobby snout.

Animals that give caimans a wide berth also tend to leave this look-alike alone. If the head fails to discourage an enemy, the insect spreads its wings and reveals startling eyespots. The lantern fly does not light up. A scientist simply misnamed it when he saw a glow around the false head. Bacteria may have caused it.

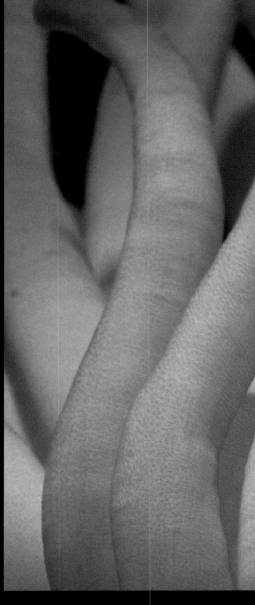

◁ *Illusion is as useful under-*
water as it is on land. In
Monterey Bay, off California,
a snubnose sculpin's coloring
matches the ocean bottom.
Its camouflage helps hide the
fish as it lies in wait for prey.
It eats small crabs, worms,
and snails.

JAMES H. CARMICHAEL, JR.

RUDIE H. KUITER/OXFORD SCIENTIFIC FILMS

△ *Fishes' friend: A delicate cleaner shrimp climbs among the armlike tentacles of a sea anemone (uh-NEM-uh-nee), a soft-bodied marine animal. The shrimp's transparent body and banded legs blend in with the color of the anemone. By waving its antennae, the shrimp attracts a variety of reef fishes. It eats parasites from their bodies and cleans wounded areas. The service is so popular that there's often quite a lineup!*

◁ *An eyespot on the fin of a young damselfish could mislead an enemy. The spot helps make the fish's rear half look like a large head. The illusion can scare off an attacker.*

79

(*Continued from page 77*)   belly blends in with the sky. A fish may not see the gull swooping down until it's too late.

Even under attack, however, some prey use illusions to make the enemy back off. The false head of the lantern fly (page 77) resembles the head of a caiman, a relative of the alligator. Predators, such as birds and monkeys, usually retreat when they see it. Even if the mimicry fails and an enemy snaps at the false head, the lantern fly may still be safe. The head is hollow. Damage to it won't cause fatal injury. The lantern fly can still fly away.

Sometimes threatening behavior makes scary markings even more effective. A kind of caterpillar found in Malaysia bluffs enemies into thinking it's a snake. It expands its front end, revealing a pair of eyespots. Then the caterpillar weaves back and forth the way certain snakes move their heads before striking. The enemy usually backs off.

O f course, not all natural illusions work all the time. If they did, the world might one day be overrun with grasshoppers, say, or viceroy butterflies. But the illusions work often enough to help certain species survive.

Scientists use the theory of natural selection to explain how animals develop camouflage and other lifesaving tricks. According to this theory, those animals that can adapt, or adjust, to their environment survive and reproduce. Animals that don't adapt die off.

Usually, scientists say, the process of natural selection takes thousands of years. Occasionally, a remarkably short time is involved. In parts of England before 1850, the gray-colored pepper moth was plentiful because of its successful camouflage. It hid on tree bark splotched with pale-colored lichens (LIE-kunz), rootless plants that live on trees and rocks. Black pepper moths were occasionally seen,

◁ *Quick-change artist: The wing cases of the Hercules beetle change color as the amount of humidity in the air changes. Here, in the daytime, humidity is relatively low. A beetle's wing cases have an orangish color. That helps the beetle hide from predators when it feeds on various kinds of fruit.*

▷ *Light-colored cases could be a handicap at night. In the damp night air, the wing cases turn dark—as these cases, caught in the photographer's flash, have done. The color switch can take just a few minutes. The beetle, one of the world's largest, has a body about the size of your fist. It lives in Central and South America.*

80

ANIMALS ANIMALS/MARTY STOUFFER

◁ *By sitting motionless in the snow, a snowshoe hare may escape detection. If an enemy is not fooled by the camouflage, the hare can spring away on large, fur-matted feet. The hare will begin to lose its white coat in the spring.*

△ *In summer, brown fur allows the snowshoe hare to blend in with thickets and forest underbrush. The animal's seasonal change of costume explains why some people call it the "varying hare."*
LEONARD LEE RUE III

Rising over a lighthouse in Massachusetts, the moon looks huge. Later, when it is high in the sky, the moon will look smaller. The size change is an illusion, of course. The moon stays the same size wherever you see it. For an explanation of this illusion, see pages 83–85.

◁ *Phantomlike, an iceberg floats on the antarctic horizon. It's a mirage—a displaced image. There is an actual iceberg, but you don't see it where it exists. The painting below shows how this mirage formed.*

▷ *Normally, light travels in a straight line. But when light rays pass through air layers of different temperatures, they curve, always toward the cooler air. The amount of curving depends on the rate of temperature change. In this scene, the solid colored lines represent three of countless rays reflected from the iceberg.*

Here, the air becomes warmer toward the water. That makes rays reflected from the berg curve upward. They enter the eye from a lower angle than the angle in which the berg actually lies. You mistakenly interpret the rays as being straight (dashed lines). As a result, the image is displaced below the actual berg. You see a mirage.

This mirage consists of an upright image of the iceberg and an upside-down image of it. A light ray from the top of the berg (solid red line) has crossed under a ray from a point lower on the berg (solid yellow line). Such crossings cause the lower image to be inverted.

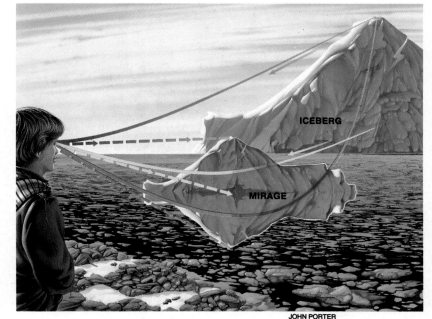

ICEBERG

MIRAGE

but were very rare. They stood out against the bark, and birds ate them.

Then factories came to England. Soot turned tree trunks black. Gray moths became easy pickings for birds. Now it was the black moths that blended in against tree bark. By 1900, black pepper moths had become plentiful; the gray variety had all but disappeared.

As a rule, human beings don't have to rely on illusion to survive in their environment. Sometimes, however, the environment plays tricks on you—as when you see a displaced image called a mirage (above) or the illusion of the moon changing size (left).

You may have noticed that the full moon looks larger when it's near the horizon than when it's high in the sky. The moon should always look the same size because it stays at the same distance and forms the same-size retinal image. Why then does its size appear to change? You will find a clue in what you learned about size scaling in chapter 1.

When the moon is overhead, there are no depth clues to help you judge its distance, so the brain assigns a distance. Tests show that most people see the overhead moon as being about a mile away and a foot across.

When the horizon is part of the scene, however, depth clues come into play. The horizon is the farthest point on earth that you

83

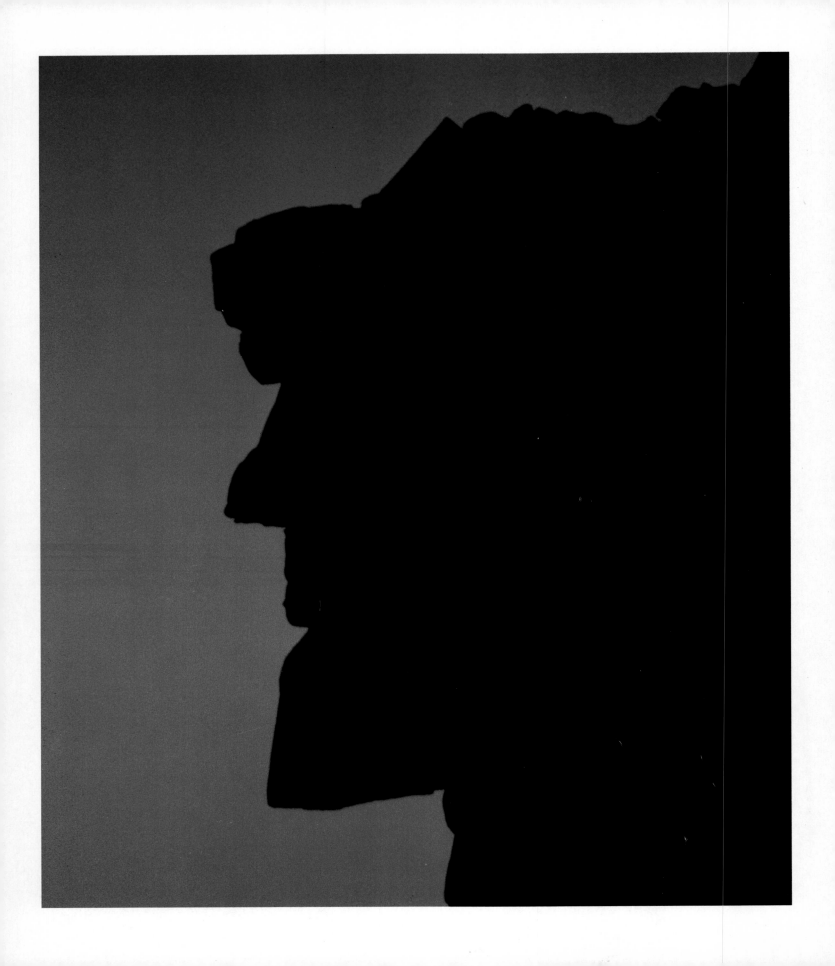

can see. Experience has taught the brain that an object's retinal image shrinks as the object moves toward the horizon. The brain corrects the shrinkage by scaling up, or increasing, its perception of size from the retinal image. That way—normally—the object's perceived size stays nearly the same.

When the moon is near the horizon, however, the brain scales up from an image that *never shrinks*. Result: The moon, with depth clues, looks larger than when it's overhead.

As for mirages, you've probably seen any number of them while riding down the highway. They probably looked like shimmering pools of water. As you approached the spots where the pools appeared to be, they vanished. Roadway mirages may not be quite so dramatic as the antarctic iceberg on page 83, but they work on the same principle.

The shimmering pools are actually images of the sky. Pavement absorbs the sun's heat and warms the air directly above the road. As light rays from the sky hit the warm air, they bend—always toward cooler air. In this case, they bend upward. If these rays reach your eyes, you see an image of the sky on the pavement. Since the heating of the air above the pavement is not uniform, the image shimmers like water.

Perhaps the most enjoyable illusions you see in nature happen in your imagination. Even after your brain has identified an object, it continues working—on overtime, you might say. It can come up with creative interpretations. It lets you see a "man" in the moon. It turns floating clouds into lambs or castles or great sailing ships. It makes a rock formation (opposite page) look like the profile of a man wearing a headband.

Working overtime, your brain can turn fact into fantasy—even when you may not be expecting it to. It's something to keep in mind next time you pass a creaking, twisted tree in the moonglow of a crisp October night.

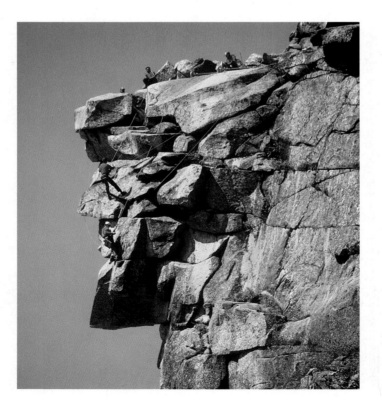

◁ *In deep shadow, a natural formation called the Old Man of the Mountain juts from a cliff in the White Mountains of New Hampshire. You know this is part of a mountain. But your brain also recognizes a familiar pattern: the profile of a face.*

▷ *Sunlight reveals the Old Man's craggy features to a group of climbers. Two surveyors are credited with discovering the profile in 1805. It was first called Jefferson. Thomas Jefferson was President at the time, and people thought the rock resembled him.*

SANDY FELSENTHAL (BOTH)

Fun With Illusions

"Your wish, sir?" A genie in a bottle greets Robbie Butilkin, 13, of Niagara Falls, Ontario, in Canada. Robbie saw the illusion—and talked to the genie—at the That's Incredible Museum in his hometown. Karen Sanduleac, 17, also of Niagara Falls, plays the genie. Officials at the museum won't tell exactly how the illusion works. They do say, though, that mirrors play a part. When visitors ask Karen how she got into the bottle, she answers: "My master, Ali Baba, put me in here because I was speeding on my flying carpet."

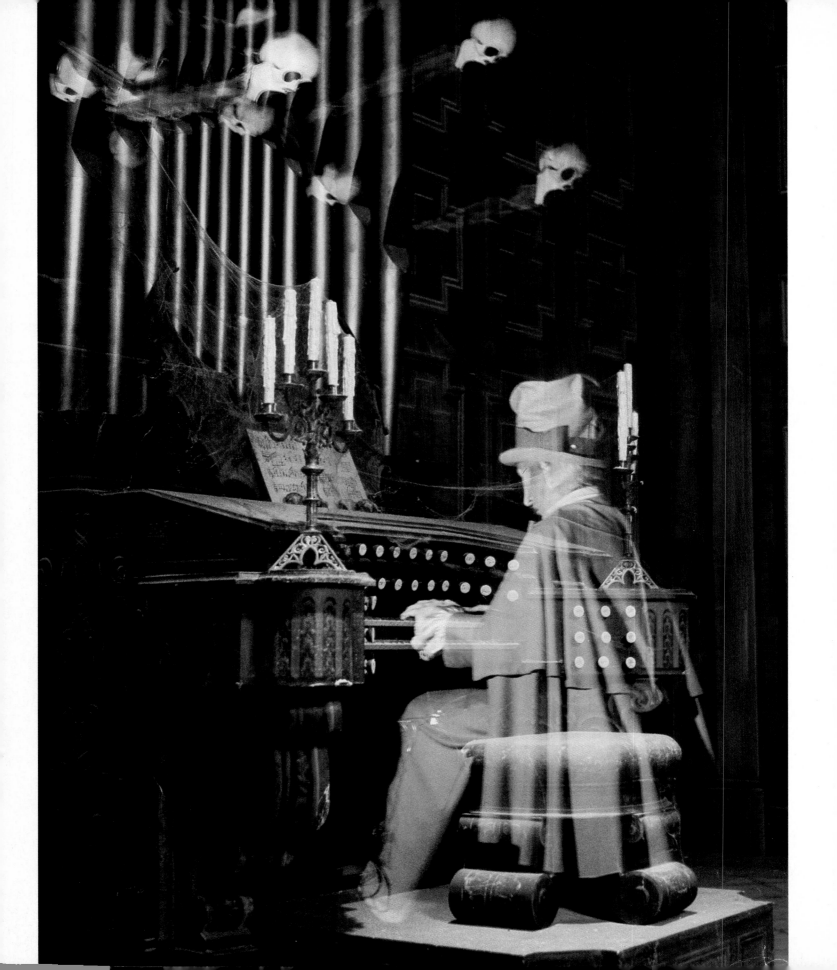

Illusion as entertainment goes back a long way. It's the basis of many magicians' tricks—and there have been magicians almost as long as there have been Egyptian, Chinese, and other major civilizations. You've probably seen a magician "sawing" a woman in half—and then magically putting her back together. A similar illusion, this one with a goose as subject, was performed in Egypt as long ago as 4000 B.C.

You'll read more about magic in the next pages. Just now, though, consider some other types of amusing illusions—fun-house mirrors, for example. The mirrors have curved surfaces that create distorted, or oddly shaped, images. You can't help chuckling at them, as you'll see on pages 96–97.

You might see another kind of entertaining illusion at large football games and other sporting events. It takes place not on the playing field but in the stands—in the card section.

One minute, a section of the stadium is filled with just another group of cheering fans. Blink an eye and that section has transformed itself into a colorful picture (pages 94–95). The picture suddenly turns into another . . . and another. It's a living billboard.

The pictures consist of large colored cards—thousands of them. On signal, the fans raise the cards. The cards form a pattern that the brain recognizes. The idea is the same as that of four-color printing, which you read about in chapter 2. Here, though, the scale is much larger.

If you should visit Walt Disney World, near Orlando, Florida, you might come across a musical ghost (opposite page). This 19th-century Englishman is only one of dozens of spirits from different times and places that inhabit the Haunted Mansion. When visitors ask exactly how many ghosts the mansion

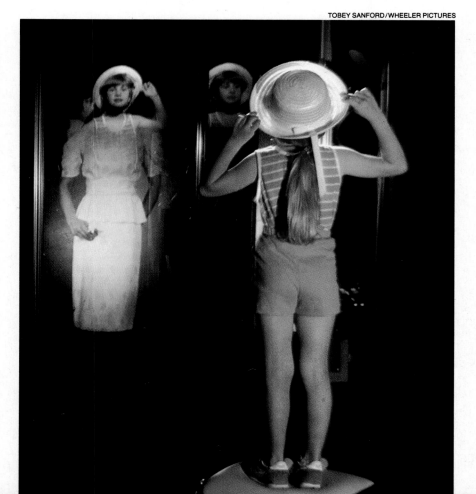

◁ As a ghostly musician plays the organ, skulls sing an eerie chorus. Visitors see—and hear—this scene at the Haunted Mansion at Disney World, near Orlando, Florida. The organist wears the hat and cape of a 19th-century Englishman. How is the spooky illusion made? Disney technicians won't say!

▷ At a clothing store in Indianapolis, Indiana, Brook Hildebrand, 9, sees how she would look in a dress without trying it on. The mirror in front of Brook reflects only the facial area. A salesclerk feeds Brook's measurements into a computer. It adjusts the proportions of selected styles to match Brook's size. Then it projects an image onto the mirror. In a flash, Brook can see how a variety of outfits will look on her.

holds, they are told: "There are 999 . . . *and there's room for one more!"*

How does he do it? The question burns in the mind of everyone who enjoys magic. A magician, though, would rather hang up his top hat for good than reveal his secrets.

"People want to be fooled," says Michael Chamberlin (left and below), a magician from Bowie, Maryland. "Most tricks are difficult to perform, but the secrets are simple. If the audience knew the secret, they'd say, 'Oh, is that all there is to it?' They'd be disappointed. The fun and mystery would be gone."

Michael, 18, has been interested in magic since he was 8. He performs at birthday parties and at other events. Usually he performs for young people. "Children are the most challenging audience," says Michael. "They haven't been taught what to believe and what not to believe. A child always wants to know how a trick works."

To help prevent an audience from figuring out a trick, Michael, like all magicians, uses misdirection. That's the art of derailing the audience's train of thought, of distracting attention away from the means by which a trick is done. The viewers mustn't know they're being misdirected. As you can guess, the technique requires good acting skills.

Magicians say that many tricks have a weak spot—a part where there's danger the audience will learn the secret. That's when misdirection comes into play. When Michael makes a coin vanish, *(Continued on page 95)*

◁ *Balancing act: A silver ball appears to rest on the edge of a silk scarf as Michael Chamberlin, of Bowie, Maryland, performs a famous trick. Like many good magicians, Michael uses facial expression to add to the effect. He stares at the Zombie Ball as if he'd never seen such an amazing sight in his life. Actually, he has practiced the trick many times. Good acting helps make magic entertaining—and convincing. Michael, 18, hopes to become an actor.*

△ *Tough trick: In another routine, Michael links and unlinks eight solid steel rings. To begin, he invites someone from the audience to inspect the rings. Inspection complete, <u>presto!</u>—Michael slaps the rings together, and they link up. Michael calls this one of his most difficult illusions. How does it work? Michael's not telling. "That," he says, "would spoil the fun."*
STEVEN ZERBY (BOTH)

91

Tricks You Can Do

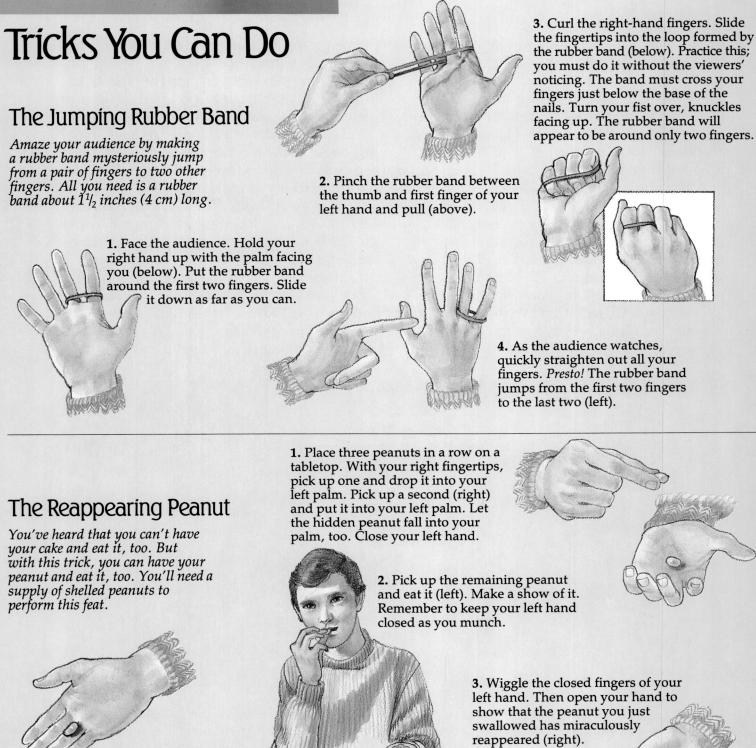

The Jumping Rubber Band

Amaze your audience by making a rubber band mysteriously jump from a pair of fingers to two other fingers. All you need is a rubber band about 1½ inches (4 cm) long.

1. Face the audience. Hold your right hand up with the palm facing you (below). Put the rubber band around the first two fingers. Slide it down as far as you can.

2. Pinch the rubber band between the thumb and first finger of your left hand and pull (above).

3. Curl the right-hand fingers. Slide the fingertips into the loop formed by the rubber band (below). Practice this; you must do it without the viewers' noticing. The band must cross your fingers just below the base of the nails. Turn your fist over, knuckles facing up. The rubber band will appear to be around only two fingers.

4. As the audience watches, quickly straighten out all your fingers. *Presto!* The rubber band jumps from the first two fingers to the last two (left).

The Reappearing Peanut

You've heard that you can't have your cake and eat it, too. But with this trick, you can have your peanut and eat it, too. You'll need a supply of shelled peanuts to perform this feat.

1. Place three peanuts in a row on a tabletop. With your right fingertips, pick up one and drop it into your left palm. Pick up a second (right) and put it into your left palm. Let the hidden peanut fall into your palm, too. Close your left hand.

2. Pick up the remaining peanut and eat it (left). Make a show of it. Remember to keep your left hand closed as you munch.

3. Wiggle the closed fingers of your left hand. Then open your hand to show that the peanut you just swallowed has miraculously reappeared (right).

TO PREPARE: Wedge a peanut between the middle and ring fingers of the right hand (above)— or the left, if you're left-handed. To look natural, let your fingers relax.

92

The Traveling Coin

In this trick, a coin magically journeys from an envelope to an empty matchbox. You may want to experiment with different sizes of envelopes to see which works best. As you work on the trick, remember that a magician also has to be an actor. For each of your tricks, develop a patter—a light, conversational speech. It makes your show more entertaining. It also distracts attention from the difficult parts of a trick.

TO PREPARE: Push a matchbox drawer about two-thirds of the way out (below). Slide a penny in the other end. Wedge it between the end of the drawer and the top of the matchbox cover.

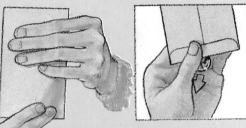

Carefully slit the side or bottom of a small manila envelope (above). Experiment with the best location for the slit. Make it a bit longer than the width of a penny. Put a second penny into your pocket.

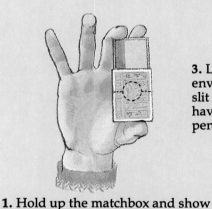

3. Lick the flap and seal the envelope (right). Take care that the slit stays concealed. You'll also have to tilt the envelope so the penny doesn't accidentally fall out.

1. Hold up the matchbox and show the empty interior to your audience (above). Slap the box down on the table to close it. The noise will cover the sound of the penny dropping.

4. This is the hard part. Practice it in private until you can perform it smoothly. Tilt the envelope so the penny slips through the slit into your hand (above). You will hide the penny in that hand as the trick continues.

5. Rip up the envelope (right). Make a big production of it. Show amazement as you "discover" there's no penny inside. Remember to keep the penny concealed in the palm of your hand.

2. Remove the penny from your pocket and show it to the audience. Drop it into the envelope (right). Gently squeeze the edges of the envelope to puff it out. Let the audience look inside to see the coin. Be sure your hand conceals the slit.

6. The finale: Pick up the matchbox and shake it. Your audience will hear the "missing" coin rattling around inside. Open the box to reveal the penny (right).

LOIS SLOAN

(Continued from page 91) he *pretends* to pass a quarter from his right hand to his left. The audience now thinks it's in the left hand. Now he has to get rid of the coin altogether—the risky part.

"I hold up my clenched left hand and stare at it dramatically," says Michael. The misdirection strengthens the illusion that the coin is in that hand. He slips his right hand into his pocket "to get some magic dust," he tells the audience—more misdirection. Now he opens both hands. The coin has vanished!

Doug Henning, who entertains audiences the world over with his magic, says actual optical illusions are used in about a third of his act. Most of the rest deals with the power of suggestion—misdirection. "What's most important," he says, "is not what the eye sees but what the mind *thinks* it sees."

Some magicians *(Continued on page 98)*

© PAUL SLAUGHTER 1987 (BOTH)

Card trick: At the 1984 Olympics, in Los Angeles, California, spectators became participants. For the opening ceremonies, they created images of the flags of each nation that took part in the games. An announcer told the crowd to find large colored cards at their seats. Then he asked the 85,000 people to raise the cards—all at once. Viewed from a distance (left), the cards make a spectacular display. Closer up (above), the illusion starts to lose its effect.

95

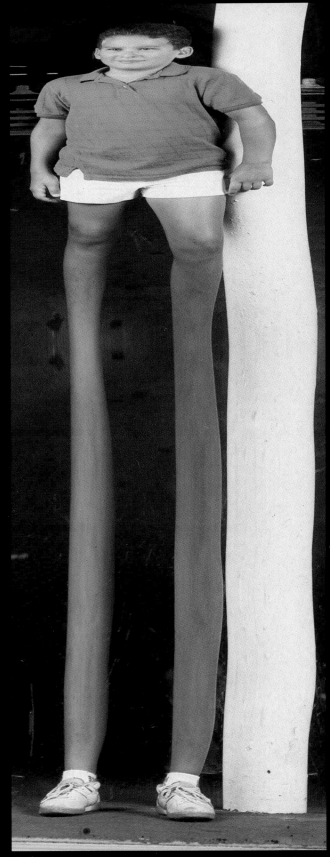

◁ *Stilt legs: Hite Billes, 11, got a new look when he went inside a mirror arcade at an amusement park in Ocean City, Maryland. Hite was visiting from New Orleans, Louisiana. "The distorted mirror," he says, "made me look like a tiny person on the top and a basketball player on the bottom."*

△ *Double Damon: One mirror makes Damon Shelton, 11, of Princess Anne, Maryland, seem to have two bodies.*

▷ *"I liked having a major neck stretch," jokes Bruce Crismond, 10, of Cambridge, Maryland. A curved surface causes the weird images in trick mirrors.*

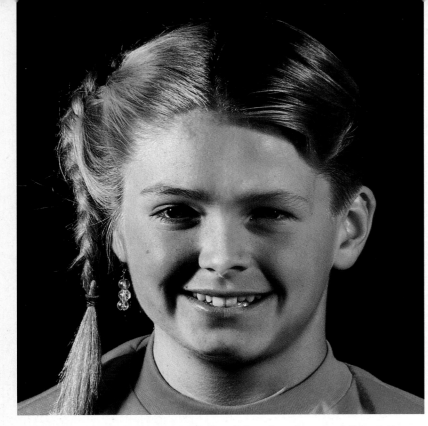

△ *Girl? Boy? Girlboy? In a hands-on exhibit at San Francisco's Exploratorium, two teenagers—a girl and a boy—join forces to combine faces.*

▽ *The exhibit uses special glass that acts as both window and mirror. By adjusting the lighting, J. D. Murray, left, of Tiburon, California, and Corina-Lenora Benjet, of San Francisco, can blend their faces in many ways. Here, with lights set for low reflection, Corina-Lenora smiles through the glass at J. D.*

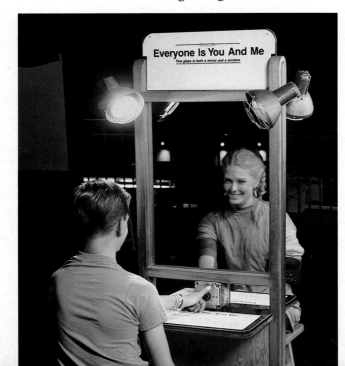

(Continued from page 95)   perform in silence. Most, however, use patter. That's small talk, the friendly chitchat that helps the act move along and aids in misdirection. It's carefully rehearsed. "For every trick, you've got to figure out a patter, tell a story," says Michael. "I keep it light and personal."

On rare occasions a trick fails onstage. An "invisible" thread breaks, or a magic box fails to open. When something like that happens, a magician has to know how to handle the situation. If a trick fails for Michael, he uses humor to turn defeat into victory. "Well, that's what happens when you study in the dark," Michael may quip, or, "*That will teach me to buy it for 39 cents!*"

Humor can also be useful in gently turning aside that burning question, "*How do you do it?*" A child asked it of Doug Henning after seeing him make colored handkerchiefs jump in and out of a bottle.

"You have to get them when they're very young," Henning replied, "and train them."

I n this book you've experienced about a hundred illusions. You have probably found some of them amusing, many informative, others pleasing, and still others just plain baffling.

If you find illusions fascinating, make a date to visit an art gallery. Art, as you discovered in chapter 2, is full of illusions. After reading the chapter, you may have found that your way of looking at paintings has changed somewhat. Your eye may be more critical, your mind more questioning.

▷ *Colors shimmer and dance in an exhibit called "Sun Painting." Sunlight streams through glass in the Exploratorium's ceiling. Prisms bend it into rainbow colors, which are bounced and scattered by mirrors. Here, the colors flicker on a frosted screen. The rule at the Exploratorium: "Please <u>do</u> touch."*

Many science museums have exhibits featuring other types of visual illusions. Often the exhibits have hands-on displays. That means you're invited to experiment with the displays for yourself.

The Distorted Room Exhibit on the cover of this book is such a display. People try it out at the Exploratorium, a museum of science, art, and human perception. It's located in San Francisco, California. Visitors to the Exploratorium can get hands-on experience at a number of displays. In one of them, two people combine their features in an endless combination of new faces.

The display is called "Everyone Is You and Me." You saw it on page 98. In the combined-faces picture, the left half of the image is a girl's face; the right half is a boy's. "We could hardly control our laughter when we glanced at each other through the glass," says the girl, Corina-Lenora Benjet, of San Francisco. "It was a weird experience."

You don't have to live in, or travel to, San Francisco to have similar experiences. Science centers—some 150 of them—are sprinkled throughout the United States and Canada. There are more in such countries as Great Britain, Mexico, India, Australia, Japan, and Thailand. They may not all feature illusions at the same time. Chances are good, though, that any one museum will run such an exhibit at some time during the year.

You'll visit the exhibit armed with a lot of information. You now know how the eye and brain work as a team. You've discovered why you experience illusions. You've seen straight lines that were really curves. You've seen an iceberg at a location where it did not exist. An organ-playing ghost? You've seen one! And you've seen an artist make water run uphill, quite believably.

"Seeing is believing," a friend might tell you, trying to convince you of something. When that happens, you'll smile. "Well, sometimes," you'll say—as you set about to show your friend a thing or two.

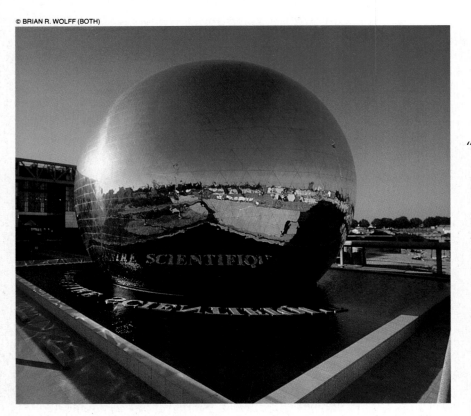

*"It's planet earth—and we haven't even left the ground." The visiting youngsters might get that impression from what they see **(right)**. They're touring the Center for Science and Industry in Paris, France. The "planet" is actually a large metal sphere **(left)**. When it reflects blue sky and fluffy clouds, and when it is seen from a certain angle, the sphere looks like earth as seen from a spacecraft. Inside it, visitors see another world of illusion—films about space, earth, and history on one of the world's largest motion picture screens.*

Index

Bold type indicates illustrations; regular type refers to text.

*In the desert near Las Vegas,
Nevada, illusionists Siegfried and
Roy—with a tiger companion—
perform a spectacular feat.
As Siegfried holds a hoop, Roy
levitates, or floats, through it.
In this setting, it would be nearly
impossible to conceal props.
Siegfried and Roy describe their
performances as filled with
"excitement, danger, razzle-
dazzle, and glamour." How they
perform their illusions remains
a carefully guarded secret.*
CHRIS CALLIS/CONTACT

Additional Reading

Readers may want to check the *National Geographic Index* in a school or a public library for related articles and to refer to the following books. ("A" indicates a book for readers at the adult level.)

Arnason, H. H., *History of Modern Art*, Abrams, 1977 (A). Barrett, Cyril, *Op Art*, Viking, 1970 (A). Beeler, Nelsen F., and Franklyn Branley, *Experiments in Optical Illusion*, Crowell, 1951. Blackstone, Harry, Jr., *The Blackstone Book of Magic and Illusion*, Newmarket, 1985. Bool, F. H., et al., *Escher*, Thames and Hudson, 1982 (A). Cobb, Vicki, *How to Really Fool Yourself*, Lippincott, 1981.

Cole, K. C., *Facets of Light*, Exploratorium, 1980. Cole, K. C., *Vision: In the Eye of the Beholder*, Exploratorium, 1978. Ernst, Bruno, *Adventures With Impossible Figures*, Tarquin, 1986. Fogden, Michael and Patricia, *Animals and Their Colors*, Crown, 1974. Froman, Robert, *Science, Art, and Visual Illusions*, Simon & Schuster, 1970.

Goldstein, E. Bruce, *Sensation and Perception*, Wadsworth, 1980 (A). Green, Peter, et al., *The Parthenon*, Newsweek, 1973 (A). Gregory, R. L., *Eye and Brain*, McGraw–Hill, 1981 (A). Gregory, R. L., *The Intelligent Eye*, McGraw–Hill, 1970 (A). Gregory, R. L., and E. H. Gombrich, (eds.), *Illusion in Nature and Art*, Scribner's, 1973 (A). Haas, Richard, *An Architecture of Illusion*, Rizzoli, 1981 (A). Heuer, Kenneth, *Rainbows, Halos, and Other Wonders*, Dodd, Mead, 1978. Kettelkamp, Larry, *Magic Made Easy*, Morrow, 1981. Kettelkamp, Larry, *Tricks of Eye and Mind*, Morrow, 1974.

Lewis, Shari, and Abraham B. Hurwitz, *Magic for Non-Magicians*, Tarcher, 1977. Manchel, Frank, *Movies and How They Are Made*, Prentice–Hall, 1968. Michell, John, *Natural Likenesses: Faces and Figures in Nature*, Dutton, 1979. Morgan, Hal, and Dan Symmes, *Amazing 3–D*, Little, Brown, 1982. Owen, Denis, *Camouflage and Mimicry*, University of Chicago, 1980. Pitman–Gelles, Bonnie, *Museums, Magic & Children*, Association of Science–Technology Centers, 1981 (A). Rainey, Patricia Ann, *Illusions: A Journey Into Perception*, Linnet, 1973. Riley, Bridget, *Working With Colour*, Arts Council of Great Britain, 1984 (A). Rock, Irvin, *Perception*, Scientific American, 1984 (A).

Sakane, Itsuo, (ed.), *The Expanding Visual World—A Museum of Fun*, Asahi Shimbun, 1979. Simon, Seymour, *Mirror Magic*, Lothrop, Lee & Shepard, 1980. Simon, Seymour, *The Optical Illusion Book*, Morrow, 1984. Smith, Thomas G., *Inside Industrial Light & Magic*, Ballantine, 1986. Thurston, Howard, *400 Tricks You Can Do*, Blue Ribbon, 1940. Unterseher, Fred, Jeannene Hansen, and Bob Schlesinger, *Holography Handbook*, Ross, 1982 (A). Ward, Peter, *Colour for Survival*, Orbis, 1979. White, Laurence B., and Ray Broekel, *Optical Illusions*, Watts, 1986.

BOOKS BY THE NATIONAL GEOGRAPHIC SOCIETY: *How Animals Behave: A New Look at Wildlife*, 1984. *The Incredible Machine*, 1986. *Messengers to the Brain: Our Fantastic Five Senses*, 1984. *Secrets of Animal Survival*, 1983. *Your Wonderful Body!* 1982.

Consultants

Richard L. Gregory, Professor of Neuropsychology, Director of Brain and Perception Laboratory, University of Bristol—*Chief Consultant*

Violet A. Tibbetts—*Reading Consultant*

Nicholas J. Long, Ph.D.—*Consulting Psychologist*

The Special Publications and School Services Division is grateful to the individuals named or quoted within the text and to those cited here for their generous assistance:

Stephen A. Benton, Massachusetts Institute of Technology; Blue Sky, Columbia, South Carolina; Tom Brinkmoeller, Walt Disney World; John Burns, National Park Service; James L. Castner, University of Florida; Michael Chamberlin, Bowie, Maryland; Clifford Chieffo, Georgetown University Art Collection; Martha L. Crump, University of Florida.

Linda Dachman, the Exploratorium; G. B. Edwards, Florida State Collection of Arthropods; John F. Eisenberg, Florida State Museum; Deborah Fine, Lucasfilm Ltd.; Dick Frank, Dick Frank Studios, Inc.

John B. Heppner, Florida State Collection of Arthropods; Isia Leviant, Paris, France; Scott Lloyd, Museum of Holography; William Loerke, Catholic University; Frank J. Maturo, Jr., University of Florida; Dennis Muren, Industrial Light & Magic; John B. O'Sullivan, Monterey Bay Aquarium; John Perkins, United Airlines Flight Center.

Charles Reynolds, Reynolds Illusion Associates; Rick Rothschild, Walt Disney Imagineering; Walter Tape, University of Alaska at Fairbanks; Winston Townsend, U. S. News & World Report; Ellen Vartanoff, Geppi's Comic World, Inc.; Andrew Vogt, Georgetown University; Charles C. Whiton, Jr., Franconia Notch State Park; William A. Xanten, Jr., National Zoological Park; Ray Zone, Los Angeles, California.

Composition for YOU WON'T BELIEVE YOUR EYES! by the Typographic section of National Geographic Production Services, Pre-Press Division. Printed and bound by Holladay-Tyler Printing Corp., Rockville, Md. Film preparation by Catharine Cooke Studio, Inc., New York, N.Y. Color separations by the Lanman-Progressive Co., Washington, D.C.; Lincoln Graphics, Inc., Cherry Hill, N.J.; and NEC, Inc., Nashville, Tenn. Teacher's Guide printed by McCollum Press, Inc., Rockville, Md.

Library of Congress CIP Data

O'Neill, Catherine, 1950–
 You won't believe your eyes!

 (Books for world explorers)
 Bibliography: p.
 Includes index.
 SUMMARY: Introduces the world of visual illusion, describing the workings of the eye-brain system and how different types of illusions occur.
 1. Optical illusions—Juvenile literature. 2. Visual perception—Juvenile literature. [1. Optical illusions. 2. Visual perception] I. Title. II. Series.
 QP495.O54 1987   152.1'48   87-7637
 ISBN 0–87044–611–8 (regular edition)
 ISBN 0–87044–616–9 (library edition)

You Won't Believe Your Eyes!

PUBLISHED BY
THE NATIONAL GEOGRAPHIC SOCIETY
WASHINGTON, D. C.

Gilbert M. Grosvenor, *President and Chairman of the Board*
Melvin M. Payne, *Chairman Emeritus*
Owen R. Anderson, *Executive Vice President*
Robert L. Breeden, *Senior Vice President, Publications and Educational Media*

PREPARED BY THE SPECIAL PUBLICATIONS
AND SCHOOL SERVICES DIVISION

Donald J. Crump, *Director*
Philip B. Silcott, *Associate Director*
Bonnie S. Lawrence, *Assistant Director*

BOOKS FOR WORLD EXPLORERS

Pat Robbins, *Editor*
Ralph Gray, *Editor Emeritus*
Ursula Perrin Vosseler, *Art Director*
Margaret McKelway, *Associate Editor*
David P. Johnson, *Illustrations Editor*

STAFF FOR *YOU WON'T BELIEVE YOUR EYES!*

Ross Bankson, *Managing Editor*
Charles M. Kogod, *Picture Editor*
Dorrit Green, *Art Director*
Catherine O'Neill, *Writer*
Suzanne Nave Patrick, *Senior Editorial Researcher*
Lucinda Moore, *Researcher*
Viviane Y. Silverman, *Preliminary Art Concept and Research*
Nancy J. White, *Editorial Assistant*
Sharon Kocsis Berry, Aimee Clause, Bernadette L. Grigonis, Karen L. O'Brien, *Illustrations Assistants*
Perry Rech, *Picture-Editing Intern*

ENGRAVING, PRINTING, AND PRODUCT MANUFACTURE: Robert W. Messer, *Manager;* George V. White, *Assistant Manager;* David V. Showers, *Production Manager;* Gregory Storer, *Production Project Manager;* George J. Zeller, Jr., *Senior Assistant Production Manager;* Mark R. Dunlevy, *Assistant Production Manager;* Timothy H. Ewing, *Production Assistant.*

STAFF ASSISTANTS: Carol R. Curtis, Katherine R. Davenport, Mary Elizabeth Ellison, Donna L. Hall, Mary Elizabeth House, Joan Hurst, Bridget A. Johnson, Sandra F. Lotterman, Eliza C. Morton, Virginia A. Williams.

MARKET RESEARCH: Mark W. Brown, Joseph S. Fowler, Carrla L. Holmes, Marla Lewis, Barbara Steinwurtzel, Marsha Sussman, Lisa A. Tunick, Judy Turnbull.

INDEX: George I. Burneston, III